BEARDOWN

THE UNIVERSITY OF ARIZONA
INTERCOLLEGIATE SPORTS—A PHOTOGRAPHIC CHRONICLE

JANET MITCHELL

Arizona
Bear Down!

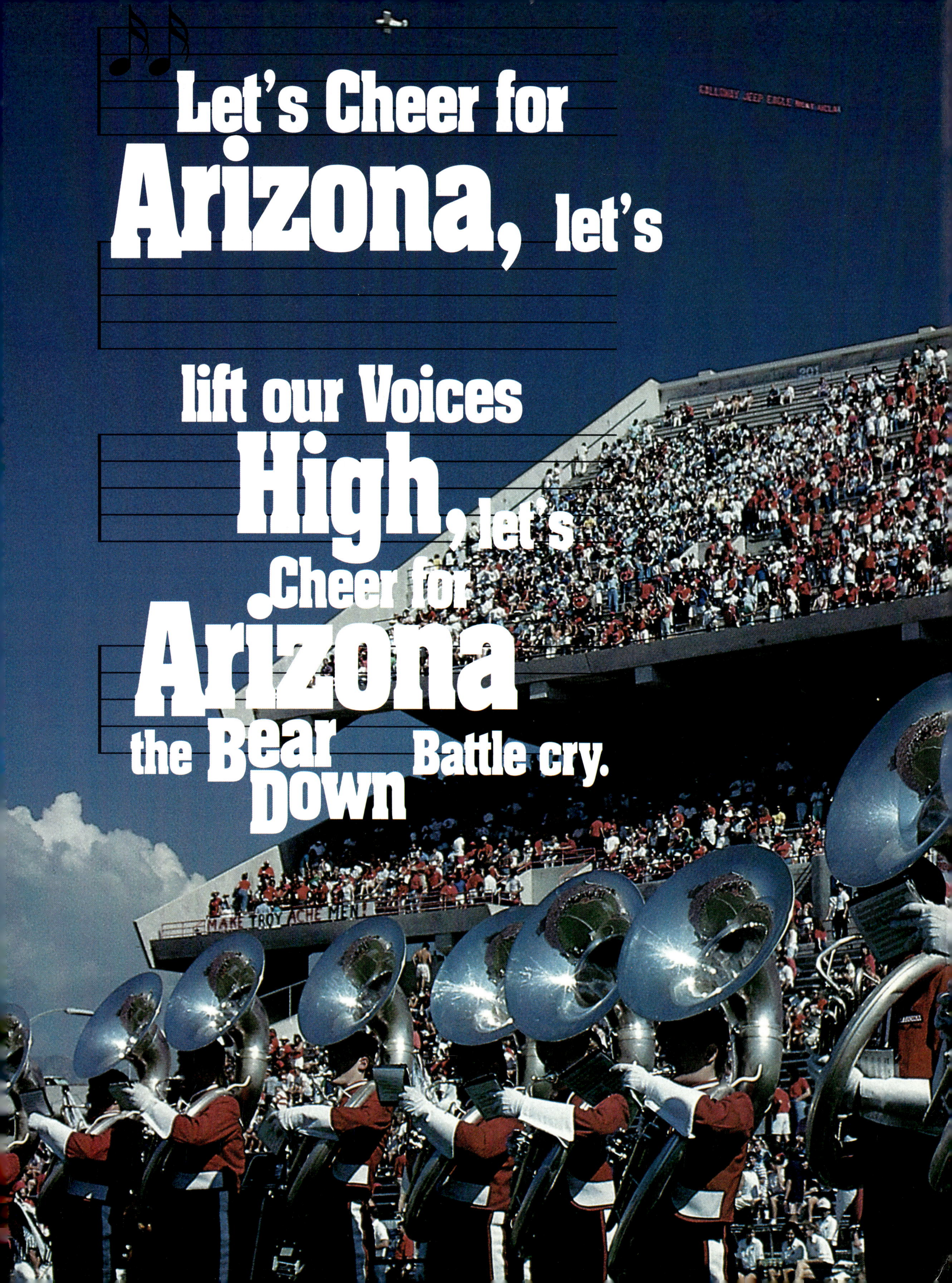

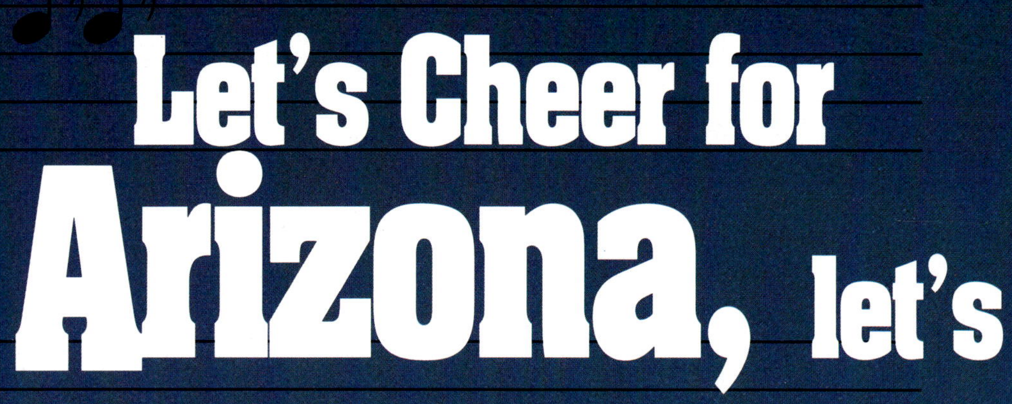

Let's Cheer for Arizona, let's lift our Voices High, let's Cheer for Arizona the Bear Down Battle cry.

MAKE TROY ACHE MEN!

Let's Cheer our Team to Victory,
Let's Cheer our Team to Fame,
Let's Cheer for Arizona, for spirit wins the game!
Bear Down, Arizona,
Bear down red and blue!

This book is dedicated to the thousands of UA men and women—both the legendary athletes and the unsung heroes on winning and losing teams—who have come to know the true meaning of "Bear Down."

Preceding pages: The UA marching band—"The Pride of Arizona"—performs prior to an afternoon contest in Arizona Stadium. *Photo: Edward McCain.*

Bear down Arizona,
Hit 'em hard, let 'em know who's who!
Bear Down, Arizona,
Go, Go Wildcats, Go! Arizona,
Arizona, Bear Down!

Contents

FOREWORD

hen it comes to sports, my passion is basketball. I would rather spend Saturday afternoon watching a college basketball game than just about anything. When the Wildcats are featured, as has happily occurred more often in recent years, I feel a sense of pride and, if the Cats win, a warmth that lasts for days. BEAR DOWN *will give us all that same warmth for years to come.*

The one constant in intercollegiate athletics at Arizona is change: from primitive facilities to state-of-the-art arenas like McKale Center, the University of Arizona can be proud of an athletic department that has usually been ahead of the change curve. The success of Arizona teams in the Pac-10 year in and year out should be a source of pride to alums everywhere.

But BEAR DOWN *does not brush off the warts and blemishes that scar athletic programs in the throes of change. I remember the story of two old grads talking in the stands, after a homecoming loss. "Let's hang the coach," says the first alum. "In effigy?" asks the second. Well, we've had some dark days at Arizona, but happily we've learned from our mistakes.*

I'd like to say here that in the postwar years I was part of a UA basketball team that went to Madison Square Garden to represent the Border Conference in the National Invitational Tournament, but after all the games that season we swept the gym and between games we washed our own uniforms and we taped our own ankles. The athletic budget during that time wasn't so spartan, but I was stunned when I saw the Wildcat locker room a few years ago when I was honorary captain in Bob Elliott's annual charity game for the minority scholarship fund. Our Bear Down gym locker room certainly had no carpeting, but it did have an aroma I'll always remember with an odd fondness.

Across the country the story is similar. Athletic programs have gone from a "mom and pop" operation to something that could only be classified as "big business." At Arizona we were lucky that our "mom" and "pop" happened to be Ina Gittings and J. F. McKale—two people who believed that athletic competition built character and that important life lessons could be learned from the experience of winning and losing. I was a student athlete. That tradition preceded me and is still there.

Now that I have left Congress and can be partisan, let me congratulate the football team on nine straight victories over ASU. My congratulations, also, to the many other Arizona teams that have achieved national recognition.

Keep up the good work and remember, "Bear Down."

Morris K. Udall
UA alumnus, member of the UA Sports Hall of Fame, and former U. S. Congressman

The leaders of Arizona have always shown a deep and persistent interest in education. An effort was made to establish a university soon after the territorial government had been organized, but it took more than 25 years for the University of Arizona to become a reality.

Acquired from Mexico as part of the Gadsden Purchase in 1854, the Arizona territory became a separate and distinct territory of the United States in 1863. At the first session of the territorial legislature held at Prescott in 1864, Governor John M. Goodwin recommended the establishment of a common school system

Framed by trees, the Memorial Fountain, and the evening sky, stately Old Main stands at the center of the University of Arizona campus, a constant link between the past and present. *Photo: Josh Young. Courtesy, University of Arizona Graphic Services.*

A TRADITION OF EXCELLENCE

The Catalina Mountains to the north and the southwestern sky provide a beautiful backdrop for the University of Arizona campus, one of the nation's best-planned and architecturally harmonious. *Courtesy, University of Arizona Athletic Department.*

Soon after UA's adoption of the nickname "Wildcats," the freshman football team gave a desert bobcat to the university. Named "Rufus Arizona" after UA president Rufus von KleinSmid, the bobcat was succeeded by many other desert bobcats until the practice of using live mascots was discontinued in the early 1960s. *Courtesy, University of Arizona Athletic Department.*

including high schools and a state university. He strongly urged that the new territory avail itself of the provisions of the Morrill Act of 1862, which provided for the establishment of an agricultural college in every state and territory.

Each succeeding governor stressed the importance of founding a university and emphasized that land grants provided by the Morrill Act would be lost if one were not established. Finally in 1885 Congress granted 72 sections of land for the use and support of an institution of higher learning in Arizona that would offer training in the agricultural and mechanical arts.

The Arizona territory was a rough and tumble place in those days and government building contracts were usually awarded on the basis of deals made in smoke-filled rooms. At the time of the 13th Territorial Legislature, the two most sought after contracts were construction of the state capitol (in Prescott) and a projected insane asylum. A university was not as appealing because, as common wisdom held at the time, "no one ever heard of a professor buying a drink."

At the time there was strong sentiment among Tucsonans for returning the capital to

Tucson. One farsighted Tucson merchant, Jacob S. Mansfeld, realized this was a political impracticality and urged the Pima County representatives to lobby instead for the location of the university in Tucson.

By the closing week of the 13th Legislature, it was decided that Phoenix would get the insane asylum and a budget of $100,000 (considered outlandish at the time), Prescott would retain the capital and Tempe would get a normal school with a budget of $5,000.

C. C. Stephens and Selim M. Franklin, two outstanding Pima County representatives, were successful in passing a university bill that located the site of the future university in Tucson and authorized a 20-year bond issue of $25,000 that became effective only if the board of regents received a gift of not less than 40 acres of land within one year.

The citizens of Tucson were not interested in having a university and loudly denounced Stephens for his part in this decision, and they called him every name in the territorial book of epithets. With time running out on the requirements of the bond issue, Mansfeld, who had been named to the board of regents, persuaded the owners of a desert site east of town to turn it over to the regents. The benefactors were two well-known gamblers of the day, E. F. Gifford and Ben C. Parker, and W. S. "Billy" Reid, who ran the best saloon in Tucson.

This charming photograph shows the university main gate, probably on an autumn Sunday, as students and faculty return from church. In a few months the wooden gates would have iron replacements and in 1916 the cement-and-brick pillars would be replaced by the black lava rock pillars still in existence today. *Courtesy, University of Arizona Athletic Department.*

On October 27, 1887, ground was broken for "Old Main," a building to be known as the School of Agriculture and Mines. Four years later the university opened with a faculty of six members and a student body of 32, only four of whom were in the college department, the remaining 28 being in the preparatory department. (In 1891 Arizona still had no public high schools.) The campus consisted of one unfinished building that contained classrooms, laboratories, faculty living quarters, the library and a well with a steam-driven pump. This solitary structure stood on 40 acres of land covered by mesquite and greasewood bushes and surrounded by a barbed wire fence.

Instruction was limited to the preparatory curriculum and courses in mines and engineering. Most of the surprisingly qualified faculty found itself precluded from teaching in their specialized fields. Mining, then the predominant industry in Arizona, was given prime attention. An agricultural experiment station was organized to take advantage of the Hatch Act of 1887, but apart from the livestock industry, agriculture had not advanced to any extent in Arizona.

Over the next twenty years UA established the quality of its education while actively participating in the development of a statewide secondary school system. In 1914 it changed from a combined college and preparatory school to one with exclusively university aims and discontinued its preparatory department. In 1915, departments of instruction were organized into three colleges: Arts and Sciences,

The University of Arizona campus, shortly after the turn of the century. *Special Collections, University of Arizona Library.*

Agriculture, and Mining and Engineering. The North Central Association of Colleges and Secondary Schools gave official recognition and membership to the university in 1917, and the American Association of Colleges received the university as a member in 1919.

Today UA is one of the top 20 public research institutions in the nation with an enrollment of nearly 37,000, a faculty and staff of 12,600 on a continually expanding 338-acre campus. Its excellent academic reputation comes from a unique blend of teaching, research and public service exemplifying the three land grant institution missions assigned to it in 1885. It excels in many fields of study, notably anthropology, philosophy, sociology, journalism, music and astronomy. The student body, representing every state and more than 90 countries, pursues degrees in 142 undergraduate, 140 master's and 109 doctoral, professional and specialist programs.

Through continued legislative support, business and industrial gifts and support from alumni and friends, as well as the many contributors to the Century II Capital Campaign, the University of Arizona, under Dr. Manuel T. Pacheco, who became its 17th president in July 1991, looks forward to continued excellence in academics, research, community service and athletics.

In the 1890s the dusty little town of Tucson offered few recreational opportunities, so the rambunctious group of college students at UA began organizing their own teams in the various collegiate sports popular at the time.

By 1896 the enrollment had reached 100, and a town team challenged the "U" boys to a track meet. In their first-recorded athletic competition, UA won all but two of the 12 events, which included a 100-yard dash, shot put, pole vault and high hurdles, as well as two bicycle

The university's first official track team competed in a track-and-field "Field Day" in 1897. The young man with the pole is Frank Groesbeck, a first-year preparatory student from Safford, Arizona, who won the pole vault event with a vault of 8' 10". *Courtesy, Special Collections, University of Arizona Library.*

WILDCAT SPORTS THEN

races and a one-mile walk.

A baseball team formed in 1898 began playing intra-class and town games and the first football team began practice in the spring of 1899. By fall of that year a student committee raised $70 from local merchants for uniforms and the team played their first scrimmage against the town, winning 5-0 (touchdowns then counting five points). The first official game, held on November 20, also against the "townies," ended in a scoreless tie.

In 1899 they took on their first collegiate opponent, Tempe Normal School (much later, Arizona State University), and inaugurated a legendary athletic rivalry. Tempe Normal won with an 11-2 victory. It is believed that several players from Tempe Normal were not even enrolled in the school, a not-uncommon occurrence at the time.

The relative geographic isolation of the school precluded a schedule of suitable opponents, so school teams competed against town teams, YMCAs, Indian schools, athletic clubs, amateur and semi-pro teams, military bases and even high schools. Not until the 1920s did collegiate opponents predominate on the schedules.

Codified rules of eligibility were generally unknown and even when existent, seldom enforced. Competent coaches were rare and paid little if anything, usually from gate receipts on a game-by-game basis. For the most part, teams were coached by enthusiastic volunteers.

NOTABLES

In the early days, UA football fans who paid for the season were not issued tickets to hand over at the gate, but buttons to wear as proof of their paid-in-full status.

Courtesy, University of Arizona Athletic Department.

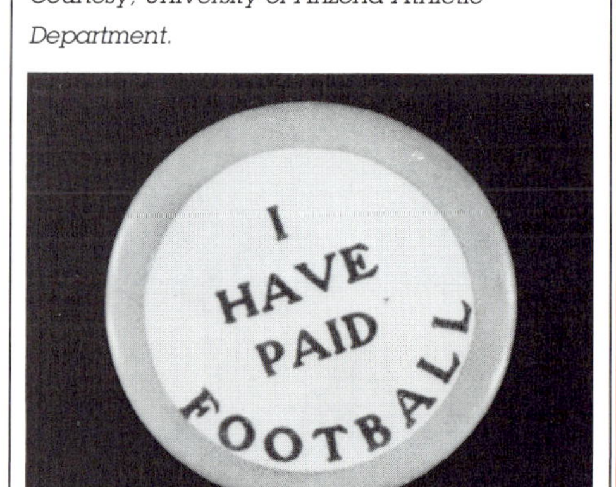

The 1905 football team was the first to travel out of state for competition, trekking to California to play Pomona College and St. Vincent's (now known as Loyola Marymount) in one of the first night games in college football history.

Baseball's first collegiate opponent was Tempe Normal in 1907. Its first out-of-state opposition came from a barnstorming Chinese team from Hawaii in 1914. Three years later they played their first collegiate match against New Mexico A&M (now New Mexico State).

Basketball, a relatively new sport, was gaining wide popularity at the turn of the century and took hold at UA in 1904 with the building of Herring Hall, the school's first gymnasium. The first collegiate opponent was Tempe Normal in 1913-14 and the team's first out-of-state trip was

against New Mexico A&M in 1916.

The Wildcat basketball team played its first out-of-state opponent in February 1930 and lost to DePaul 29-16 in Bear Down Gym. Four years later the Basketcats made their first road trip out of the adjacent state area, playing eight games in 11 days in six states from Oklahoma to Indiana.

Other sports began joining the Wildcat athletic lineup in the 1920s. Polo, as an adjunct to the Army ROTC cavalry training program, was established as a sport in 1921 and played until 1942 when mechanized armor replaced horses in warfare. Swimming made a brief appearance from 1928-30 and returned for good after the war. Boxing achieved varsity status from 1934-38 and golf was established in 1935. Fifty-seven years later, in 1992, UA won its first NCAA golf title!

Asa Porter sweeps right for Arizona. Porter transferred to the UA in 1914 from Atlanta's Emory College, which did not have a football team. However, as a gifted natural athlete, Porter took to the sport instantly. *Courtesy, the Asa Porter Family.*

Following World War II a number of new sports came and went, including riflery, wrestling, gymnastics, fencing, lacrosse and water polo. Swimming and cross-country, which achieved varsity status in 1958, are the only new postwar sports to survive into the 1990s.

Easily the standout Arizona athlete of the territorial era was Burrell Hatcher who, thanks to the liberal eligibility rules of the day, earned 18 letters in sports—football (four), basketball (two), baseball (seven) and track (five)—between 1903 and 1910, captaining seven teams. He later served two separate terms as president of the Arizona Alumni Association and was inducted into the UA Sports Hall of Fame in 1985.

Arizona passed from territorial status to statehood on February 14, 1912. Two years later a golden era of men's athletics began at the

University of Arizona.

In 1914, J. F. "Pop" McKale, the University of Arizona's "grand old man" of athletics, was hired away from Tucson High after a letter-writing campaign by university supporters. When he took over, there was no real gymnasium, athletic equipment was scarce and outdoor sports were played on a rocky lot in back of Old Main.

Financial support for athletic programs was tenuous at best. For the 1915 school year, McKale was granted appropriations of $575 to run the football program, $200 for basketball, $40 for tennis, $10 for track and $10 for baseball. His salary to coach all men's sports and serve as athletic director was $1,700 a year.

McKale's first year as head football coach was a landmark year for Arizona. The team gained the nickname "Wildcats" after a hard-fought loss to West Coast powerhouse Occidental College. That same season Arizona defeated another West Coast titan, Pomona College, for the Southwest Championship. In 1915 school pride in Arizona athletics propelled construction of a giant block "A" on Sentinel Peak west of town.

New Mexico defeated Arizona 23-11 in the 1909 territorial football battle. The winner's trophy was awarded by famous orator and politician William Jennings Bryan, whose son was a UA sophomore. Note the buggies and horseless carriages parked right next to the field. *Courtesy, Special Collections, University of Arizona Library.*

World War I curtailed Arizona athletics for a few years but brought military athletic equipment to campus. Nearly half of all college athletes received commissions and only four percent of all college students received similar rank. The UA's 1916 football team serves as an example: out of 16 lettermen, 11 became officers.

The Arizona football team gained national attention in 1921 when it was chosen to play then-national power Centre College of Kentucky in the first East-West Christmas Classic post-season bowl game on December 26 in San Diego. Although the Wildcats lost 38-0 in a sea of mud, the UA basketball and baseball teams had begun to show well against the more prominent West Coast schools.

Prior to UA's 1917 contest with USC at the Trojan's Bovard Field, Coach J. F. McKale, standing left, gives pre-game instructions to his Wildcats. USC prevailed 31-6. *Courtesy, University of Arizona Athletic Department.*

Sweeping new developments took place in 1925 when McKale was elevated to the official position of director of athletics and additional coaches were hired. Fred Enke, a football and basketball star at Minnesota and former head coach at Louisville, was hired to take charge of basketball and Walter Davis took over track and field. These men also served as assistant football coaches under McKale.

Another milestone occurred in 1925 when a regularly scheduled home football game made money. A net profit of $19.25 was shown for the game against Tempe State Teachers College (formerly the Tempe Normal School).

As student enrollment and participation in athletics grew, the need for new facilities became apparent. The first gymnasium on campus, Herring Hall, built in 1904, had become completely inadequate as well as dangerous to play in and could seat only a few hundred cramped spectators at one end. Beginning in 1922 home games were played in the city armory and at Tucson High School.

In November 1925 a $130,000 contract was let for construction of the new "Men's Gym."

A torrential downpour the night before and during the 1921 Christmas Classic completely nullified Arizona's Slonaker-led passing attack and thus spelled doom for the Wildcats. Led by All-America quarterback Bo McMillan and several other All-America and all-region players, Centre College used its powerful running attack to submerge the Cats, 38-0. Here, Arizona's defense attempts to gang-tackle McMillan. *Courtesy, University of Arizona Athletic Department.*

NEW COACH J. F. McKALE HIRED IN 1914

Sometime in 1897 in Lansing, Michigan, deputy sheriff William H. McKale salvaged a worn punching bag from the officers' gym and gave it to his 10-year old son, James, who promptly cut off the straps and introduced football to his friends.

Because he owned the ball, McKale was team coach, captain and quarterback. It was an auspicious beginning for the future dean of Arizona coaches. McKale played baseball and football in high school and football at Albion College in Michigan.

He began coaching at Superior High School in Wisconsin and in 1911 moved to Tucson to coach the high school football and baseball teams winning state championships in both his first year.

In 1914 a group of Arizona students, tired of losing to Tucson High, launched a letter-writing campaign and convinced the UA administration to hire McKale.

In 1917 he was hired to coach all teams at the UA, ushering in a new era of athletics. McKale was instrumental in improving the athletic facilities and bringing Arizona to today's outstanding athletic reputation.

McKale was known for his humor and practical jokes. On a train trip to USC, he heard that one of his players had never been out of Arizona. He had a porter wake the player when they reached the Salton Sea to tell him it was the Pacific Ocean. The youth gazed out his window, enthralled at discovering the "Pacific." From then on his teammates called him "Balboa."

McKale left coaching in 1949 to devote himself full time to his duties as athletic director. He retired in 1957 but remained active as athletic director emeritus until his death in 1968.

J. F. "Pop" McKale at football practice in 1914. ***Courtesy, Special Collections, University of Arizona Library.***

Completed in time for fall classes in 1926, what soon came to be known as "Bear Down Gym" was a showcase facility of its day, featuring a hardwood court, seating capacity for over 4,000, office space, extensive shower and locker room facilities and a 40-by-60-foot exercise, conditioning and gymnastics room. More than 3,000 people attended the inaugural game on January 27, 1927, as UA defeated Tempe State Teachers College 29-18.

The expansion of the UA's athletic plant continued with construction of a new football stadium getting underway in March 1929 as part of a $170,000 package that included the football field and a stadium seating 8,000, a quarter-mile track, two practice fields, a baseball field and stadium seating 1,300 and a swimming pool located behind Bear Down Gym. The first game in the new stadium was played October 11, 1929, a 35-0 victory over Cal Tech. By 1930 the University of Arizona could confidently boast of having the best physical plant for athletics in the Rocky Mountain-Southwest area and one of the finest overall in the entire western half of the United States.

The men's intercollegiate sports program at the UA took a major step forward to national recognition and acceptance on April 10-11, 1931, when five southwest schools met in Tucson to form the Border Intercollegiate Athletic Conference. In addition to Arizona, founding members included

Arizona State College at Tempe, Arizona State College at Flagstaff, New Mexico and New Mexico State. Texas Tech joined in 1932, followed in 1935 by Texas Western (now Texas-El Paso), and in 1941 the addition of West Texas State and Hardin-Simmons University brought conference membership to nine.

During the 1950s Border Conference schools began to seek other alignments, leading to the league's eventual dissolution in 1962. By the late 1950s burgeoning enrollments and growth of athletic programs at Arizona and Arizona State were rapidly outpacing the Border Conference's smaller schools, and discussions had begun concerning the formation of a new league. Arizona officially withdrew from the Border Conference in 1961 and ASU's withdrawal the following year resulted in the ultimate demise of the Border Conference.

During its 30 years of membership in the Border Conference, despite winning only three league football crowns, Arizona dominated competition, winning a total of 64 team titles, more than twice as many as any other school.

Although the earliest record of women's organized athletics dates back to the turn of the century, it took nearly 80 years and a federal regulation known as Title IX before women were to receive full acceptance in athletics at the University of Arizona.

"Bear Down" Legend Becomes a Great Arizona Tradition

The Wildcats' battle cry of "Bear Down" comes from the dying words of a popular student-athlete. John "Button" Salmon was president of the student body, starting quarterback and three-year catcher for the baseball team. Nicknamed for his small frame (5'8", 145 pounds) and impish good looks, he was very popular with his teammates, coach and fellow students.

The year before his death, Salmon had dazzled 30,000 Trojan fans at USC with his powerful punts and fearless defensive play. The recklessness of this hard-rock kid with the curly, reddish hair inspired his teammates to nickname him "The Leaping Tuna."

Salmon was also a talented baseball catcher. In the spring of 1925 his clutch two-base hit drove in the winning run against USC. When he was elected student body president a few days later, he referred to that hit as "the 200-vote double."

The day after the 1926 season's opening game, Salmon was driving with three friends when he missed a treacherous curve and spun over a ravine. Although the others were not seriously injured, he suffered a serious spinal cord injury and died on October 18, 1926, at St. Mary's Hospital. His final message to his teammates, given to coach McKale, who visited Salmon every day in the hospital, was "Tell them...tell the team to bear down."

At Salmon's funeral service, a three-mile line of cars snaked from downtown Tucson to the cemetery.

A year later the student body voted to make "Bear Down" the official slogan of all Wildcat teams and in 1939 the State of Arizona issued a proclamation declaring the phrase "Bear Down" to be the sole and exclusive property of the University of Arizona.

In 1926 there was no one on campus more popular than Bisbee's John "Button" Salmon. ***Courtesy, Special Collections, University of Arizona Library.***

Prior to the football fields being properly seeded and grassed in the early 1920s, UA coeds had the "honor" of clearing the field of rocks and other hazards. *Courtesy, University of Arizona Athletic Department.*

WOMEN'S SPORTS

During the early 1900s women were trained to be genteel and restrained. Elsa Chapin, the first women's director of physical training at the University of Arizona, said that "attractive womanhood, not physical strength" was the aim of the department. Emphasis was placed not upon competition, but on carriage and grace. However, as women participated in games and sports, the concept of physical training beyond calisthenics began to be realized.

In 1912 university women requested the formation of an intercollegiate basketball team. This request was denied because of a ruling by the faculty that forbade all "outside games" for women students. The university's first commitment to sports for women was in 1916, when the 4:30-6:00 p.m. time period was set aside for their daily active participation in intramurals.

Real growth in women's sports did not begin until Ina Gittings arrived on campus in 1920 as director of physical education for women and founded the UA Women's Athletic Association (WAA). Gittings was to women's sports at the University of Arizona as "Pop" McKale was to men's sports.

The first WAA meeting was held on January 12, 1921. At this meeting it was proposed that "A" letter sweaters be awarded to women who had earned a specified number of points through their participation in intramural sports. This received the Associated Students' approval only on the condition that it be distinguished from the men's athletic letter by enclosing the "A" within a circle.

The creation of a women's "A" Club in 1922 served to recognize outstanding sportswomen who had accumulated more than 1,000 points through participation in WAA activities. In the fall of 1958 the WAA became the Women's Recreation Association (WRA) and continued to oversee women's athletics through the 1973-74 school year. In 1974 the Arizona Board of Regents approved the awarding of athletic scholarships to women and the Department of Women's Intercollegiate Athletics was established, with Dr. Mary Pavlich Roby, as the school's first women's athletic director.

In perhaps the earliest known photo of women's athletic activity at the university, these ladies line up before a basketball game on an outdoor court. Uniforms were mandatory for women in the early years. (Note the backboards made of screen material.) *Courtesy, Special Collections, University of Arizona Library.*

In 1963 the Arete Society had been initiated by Roby, and for 14 years until its disbandment in 1978, when women became eligible for varsity athletic letter awards identical to those earned by male athletes, the navy blue Arete Society blazer was the only distinctive letter award that could be earned by women athletes.

Marguerite Chesney, who joined Gittings in 1922 and succeeded her as women's physical education director in 1951, was the pioneer of women's tennis at the university. Known as "Miss Tennis" in southern Arizona, Chesney for years held nearly every women's singles title in the southwest.

At first the women's physical education classes and some WAA activities were held on the second floor of Old Main. When Bear Down Gym was built to house the men's programs, the women's programs were moved into Herring Hall.

Tired of having her department shuffled

SCHOOL COLORS

The official colors of the University of Arizona were originally sage green and silver. But in 1898 student manager Quintus J. Anderson was offered a set of solid blue football jerseys trimmed in red at an extremely low price. The team needed new jerseys and had very little money, so Anderson accepted the offer.

The colors of the new jerseys were enthusiastically accepted by the Arizona athletes, students and administration. Almost immediately red and blue were approved as the new school colors. While many shades of the colors have been used over the years, UA's official colors are cardinal red and navy blue.

Pictured are: 1900 football coach, Quintus J. Anderson, left, team captain Courtland "Pike" Day, center, and coach W. W. Skinner, right. ***Courtesy, Special Collections, University of Arizona Library.***

While most athletic activity for UA women in the early 1900s consisted of exercises and drills, there were occasional departures from the monotony. Here, a group of bloomer-clad coeds, short on formal and proper running attire but no doubt long on enthusiasm, crossed the finish line at the end of a race. *Courtesy, University of Arizona Athletic Department.*

from one part of campus to another, Gittings finally convinced the administration of the need for a modern, permanent physical education plant for women. The first women's field, located where the Administration Building now stands, was followed by the construction of the Women's Physical Education Building in 1935.

By the early 1960s women's physical education had long outgrown its facilities. Plans already underway for the expansion of the Student Union had doomed the first "Women's Building," and construction of buildings in the new "inner campus" would soon eliminate the women's playing fields. In December 1964 women's physical education moved into a spacious new building, featuring two gymnasiums, a competition swimming pool and expanded office and administrative space, located on the east side of Cherry Avenue. On April 10, 1985, that building was renamed the Ina E. Gittings Building, becoming the first building on campus to be named after a female faculty member.

In 1923 the WAA petitioned the UA president for permission to compete with other colleges. The first women's intercollegiate game was played in basketball against Tempe Normal in Herring Hall that same year. Receiving permission to compete was in itself a joyous victory for the UA women. However, it brought with it an increasing concern for financing future events of the WAA. An editorial in the *Wildcat* that ran on December 20, 1923, read:

"Every student at the University of Arizona pays $5 at registration. The fund this forms is large enough to provide for eight intercollegiate football games, BUT it shrinks amazingly when girls ask for intercollegiate athletics of any kind. We have three football coaches this year, but when the women of the university ask for one hockey coach for three weeks at the cost to the university of $10, their request is ruled out. These are only two examples of the constant fight the women have to wage to have any sort of athletics at all. Women's athletics mean athletics for all, whereas men's athletics means a few teams representing a very small percentage of the men of the student body. The women of the University of Arizona have a right to protest against the injustice and one-sidedness of the present system."

Frozen in mid-leap in 1917, this UA coed managed to clear the high jump bar while gazing at the camera. This picture was taken just east of Agriculture Hall. Ten years later, Bear Down Gym would stand on the spot occupied by the buildings in the background. *Courtesy, University of Arizona Athletic Department.*

GREAT MOMENTS

Ina E. Gittings Establishes the Women's Athletic Association in 1921

Ina E. Gittings
Courtesy, Special Collections, University of Arizona Library.

Seventy years ago Ina Gittings facilitated the development of a women's athletic program at the University of Arizona. Today the Arizona Technology Development Corporation (ATDC) facilitates successful commercialization of technology developed at the UA. A wholly owned subsidiary of the University of Arizona Foundation, ATDC works with the Office of Technology Transfer to ensure that invention disclosures, technology transfer enabling disclosures, patents, and licensing issues are dealt with properly. The success of any venture depends on active participation and careful planning by the key individuals. The forward-thinking Ina Gittings set the foundation of today's successful UA physical education and athletic programs for women. Similarly ATDC provides professional support and incubator services to help the founders of start-ups create a successful venture from the beginning.

Ina Estelle Gittings was director of Physical Education for Women at the University of Arizona for 31 years. She contributed as much to the educational mission of the UA as any individual in the institution's history. Gittings' basic and consuming interest was to develop in young women a consciousness of good health, as well as the means to achieve and preserve it.

Gittings initiated the idea of "sports" in physical education in addition to the traditional classes in formal gymnastics. In 1921, the year following her hire, she founded the Women's Athletic Association, which included extracurricular activities of intramural sports and dance clubs. She also promoted the involvement of the student officers of WAA in conferences on the regional and national levels. When Gittings retired in 1951, a majority of women students at the university had participated in WAA programs.

When Ina (pronounced "Ena") Gittings came to the UA in 1920, she made up the entire women's physical education faculty. In her first year she had 150 students. When Gittings retired 31 years later, there were 1,252 women students enrolled in physical education department courses that were taught by a faculty of 10 women.

When Gittings was hired, the extent of the department's facilities consisted of one upstairs room in Old Main for classroom instruction, the floor space across the hall for games and four dirt tennis courts. By the early 1930s Gittings had nearly 500 students registered for physical education classes, and the available facilities were inadequate to meet their needs.

She kept eyeing the university vegetable garden and thinking what a nice athletic field it would make. Finally Gittings went to the administration and said, "Which is more important—cabbages or coeds?" The coeds won, and it was the beginning of the extensive physical education facilities women enjoy today.

Gittings was born in 1885 in Wilber, Nebraska. She graduated from the University of Nebraska with an A.B. degree in 1906 and from the University of Arizona with a M.A. degree in 1925. She did postgraduate work at Columbia University from 1929 to 1930. Prior to her arrival at the UA, she taught at the University of Nebraska (1907-1917) and the University of Montana (1917-1918).

The physical education program Gittings developed for women at the UA included classes for the disabled and girls in ill health. Those who could not participate physically enrolled in a classroom health course. For those able to participate in lighter exercise, golf and croquet were substituted for basketball, hockey, swimming and horseback riding.

Gittings enjoyed the outdoors, and homesteaded a desert area north of town, approximately 1.5 miles west of Oracle Road, on what was to become Ina Road. But like most others, Gittings maintained a residence downtown. The homestead was a getaway place, often used as a fun rendezvous for the students and faculty Gittings invited for the desert steak fries.

Gittings turned over the reins to the women's physical education department to Marguerite Chesney in 1951 but continued to serve as a professor of physical education until 1955. In a speech she gave at the time of her retirement, Gittings stated that the objectives she had strived to maintain were recreative physical exercise (not monkey drills), clean-cut competition, and acknowledgment of mental acumen in the midst of play and physical activity.

Gittings also stressed the need for instructors to continue teaching the basic skills of the various sports taught in the department. "A girl cannot fully enjoy a sport until she can do it well," Gittings said.

In 1985 the faculty and administration of the UA paid a special tribute to the uniqueness, achievements and wisdom of Ina Gittings. They renamed the physical education building the Ina E. Gittings Building. It was the first building on the campus to be named for a woman who was also a member of the UA faculty.

Many debates took place before the organization began to receive some financial consideration from the Associated Students Organization in 1924.

Under the direction of Ina Gittings, the WAA program flourished. In addition to intramurals, various clubs such as the Desert Mermaids, Putters, Desert Riders and the Racquet Club developed. Some of these clubs provided occasional opportunities for women to compete with other schools.

In 1924 a women's shooting team formed and arrangements were made to hold telegraphic matches with other universities. The most novel match of the season was staged between the men's team and the women's team with a dinner at the Santa Rita Hotel as a prize to the winners. The men lost and picked up the tab!

In 1925 the women's baseball team scheduled their first games with an outside team. Two games were played with Tempe Normal with the UA losing 28-18 in the first match but staging a comeback and defeating the Normals in the second game.

Throughout the years, the amount of financing for women's sports determined the extent of the competition the program could provide. In 1943-44 the UA allotted the women athletes a budget of approximately $1,500 to support five sports. Thirty years later (1973-74) the budget amounted to $35,000 with intercollegiate competition held in 12 sports.

QUOTABLES

"Your word is your bond,' and 'persistence and determination are the keys to success' were lifelong beliefs formed by the experiences our father, James H. Hearon, as the first field captain of the University of Arizona Polo Team. The UA Polo Team he led from 1924 to 1926 lost only to Princeton in the 1924 national championship and to Pennsylvania in 1926. This earned him early induction into the UA Sports Hall of Fame. It also served him in his successful career as founder of Hearon Realty and Mortgage Company and the first president of the Arizona Real Estate Board in 1948. These principles have been etched into our lives, and we are passing them along to future generations."

JAMES H. HEARON III,
WILLIAM W. HEARON AND DUFF C. HEARON

The evolution of women's intramurals and clubs into a full-fledged program of intercollegiate athletics would not have been possible without the dedicated efforts of women such as Gittings, who retired in 1951, and Chesney, as well as Mary Pilgrim and Donna Mae Miller, who continued their pioneering efforts as directors of the Department of Physical Education for Women. These women also made a contribution to the women's sports program—Chesney in tennis, Pilgrim in WAA and archery, and Miller in tennis.

When Mary Pavlich Roby was handed the reins of the WAA in 1960, its name had changed to the Women's Recreation Association (WRA). During the 1960s, in addition to the traditional and continuously popular intramural program, the club sports program began to expand its competitive

Polo Team Brings UA Athletics First National Recognition

The University of Arizona has received its share of athletic glory in recent years, but it still savors the national recognition brought to it by its legendary polo teams.

Polo brought color and spectacle to the UA unmatched by any other sport from the 1920s until the outset of World War II. The UA polo teams were among the best in the country and were recognized by presidents, senators, congressmen and show people.

Colonel R.M. Parker introduced the game to the UA in 1922 with a string of eight motley horses, some mallets and a few balls. The first polo games were played on the military parade grounds, where Arizona Stadium is today. By 1925 the team was playing its games on the Santa Catalina polo field, the present site of the University Medical Center.

After just one year, the UA team routed the championship team of Stanford University, said to have the best college team on the west coast. And in 1930-31 and 1931-32 the Wildcats put together seasons of 36-3 and 28-7 and toured the nation, defeating New Mexico Military Institute, Stanford, Oklahoma, Ohio State and the U.S. Military Academy at West Point.

Because the UA team couldn't take its horses along, it was forced to beg or borrow mounts for games in the East, prompting the Eastern newspapers to dub them the "polo team on wheels" or "the horseless polo team." But the trip was an overwhelming success—of the 10 school games played, Arizona lost only to Yale.

Because of funding, the game was discontinued in 1942, ending an athletic era and a decade in which the Wildcats ruled as the western collegiate champions.

The 1924 polo team, captained by Jimmy Hearon, second from right. *Courtesy, Special Collections, University of Arizona Library.*

Team captain James "Jimmy" Hearon moved in for a shot during this 1923-24 game. Although he was "at back" or a defenseman, Hearon was a potent goal-scorer. Below: Arizona's opponent in this 1933 match featured some former UA players and film stars. *Courtesy, University of Arizona Athletic Department.*

schedule. The WRA sponsored 12 clubs and most managed some dual state and regional tournaments.

There were even some sports in which national tournaments were sponsored for individuals and teams. A little known fact is that the school's first national collegiate title was won in 1955 by a UA women's team at the National Intercollegiate Pocket Billiards Championships. In a nationwide telegraphic match, the three-woman UA team outscored second place Purdue 110-69 and Judy Ferles won the individual title.

But a governing body to oversee all women's collegiate

Right: Ina Gittings in her undergraduate days at Nebraska. Gittings believed women's athletics should go well beyond calisthenics and exercises. *Courtesy, Special Collections, University of Arizona Library.*

sports was still a long way from becoming a reality.

In the fall of 1971, Dr. Roby was named the first director of Women's Intercollegiate Athletics at the UA. Her participation and leadership in sports as an undergraduate had prompted a continuing interest in the administrative aspect of (and eventually, men's) athletics at the collegiate level. The final Title IX Regulation Implementing Education Amendments of 1972, prohibiting sex discrimination in education, became effective in July 1975, and institutions throughout the nation were expected to be in compliance by 1978. This inspired phenomenal growth of women's athletics.

There were plenty of wide open spaces not far from campus in the 1920s, and Ina Gittings' equestrian groups covered many of them. Here, some university coeds thunder across a dry wash. *Courtesy, University of Arizona Athletic Department.*

Dr. Roby's appointment as Director of Women's Intercollegiate Athletics coincided with the passage of Title IX, which called for gender equity in all aspects of education, including athletics. It was an important piece of federal legislation that would forever change the shape of women's sports at the UA and throughout the nation.

In 1970 Arizona joined the Intermountain Athletic Conference (IAC) which included schools in Arizona, Colorado, New Mexico, Utah, Wyoming and west Texas.

In the fall of 1971, the Association of

Intercollegiate Athletics for Women (AIAW) became the first national organization to conduct women's championships and the UA women's athletic program became a charter member and an active participant. The AIAW sponsored championships in badminton, basketball, fencing, field hockey, golf, gymnastics, softball, swimming and diving, tennis, track and field and volleyball. Cross country was initiated, and synchronized swimming was added in 1976.

Arizona's fledgling women's intercollegiate program got off to a quick start, capturing the 1971 Southern California Intercollegiate Fencing Championship title in Los Angeles, placing second nationally in golf and winning conference and regional titles in gymnastics in 1972. Golf also finished fourth and seventh, respectively in 1973 and 1974, gymnastics 11th in 1973, softball seventh and swimming 16th in 1974.

In 1975 the University hosted its first women's national championship, staging the AIAW Intercollegiate Golf Championship Tournament at Oro Valley Country Club, June 16-21.

True varsity sports for women at the UA had begun in 1974-75 with the awarding of the first partial athletic scholarships to women and the merging of women's PE and the WRA with men's PE and men's athletics in the newly created Department of Physical Education and Athletics.

In 1977-78 the first full scholarships became available to women and by 1980, the athletic budget for women had increased more than fivefold. The number of women athletes receiving financial aid had grown from a handful to more than 100.

In 1981, physical education and the intercollegiate sports program were finally separated once and for all, creating a basic organizational structure that exists today, an independent Department of Intercollegiate Athletics in charge of all men's and women's sports.

The competitive success of the UA women's teams in the AIAW during the late 1970s and into the early 1980s reflected the school's increased support. Before being discontinued in 1980, field hockey won conference and regional titles in 1977 and 1978, placing 13th and 14th, respectively, nationally. The softball team was runner-up in the 1977 College World Series and won the confer-

NOTABLES

Arizona Stadium was dedicated on October 12,1929, at the Homecoming game against Cal Tech. The Wildcats inaugurated their new arena in splendid fashion by burying Tech 35-0. Here is a ticket from that historic game.

Courtesy, University of Arizona Athletic Department.

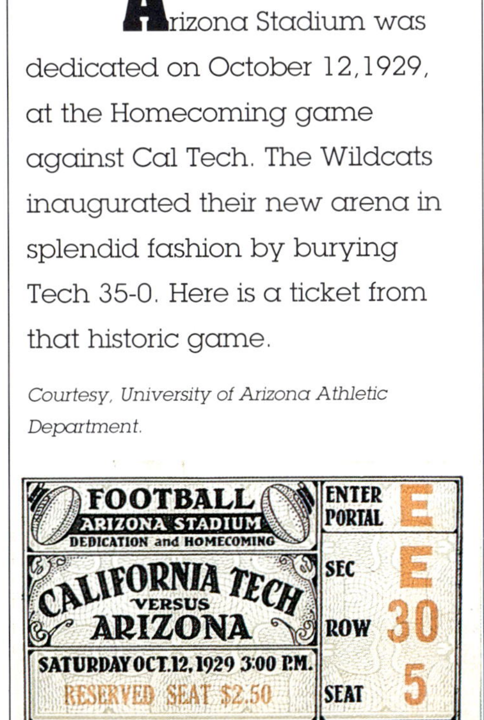

By 1905 the women's uniforms had become more nautical in nature, though no more suitable for athletic activity. Sports for women in 1905 consisted primarily of calisthenics and military-style drilling. *Courtesy, Special Collections, University of Arizona Library.*

ence title in 1979. The UA golf team won the IAC title in 1978 and recorded four straight national top-10 finishes from 1976-79. Volleyball was ranked ninth nationally in 1978 and won the league championship in 1979. Swimming finished fifth nationally in 1975 and in 1978 Diane Johnson became the UA's first AIAW national champion, winning the 400-yard individual medley.

Synchronized swimming, which was discontinued in 1985, placed third in 1978, second in 1979 and won the first of its three national team titles, tying for first in 1980. Track and cross country, initiated in 1976-77, had become national powers by the beginning of the 1980s.

The late 1970s and early '80s also saw major

Mary Roby: UA's First Director of Women's Athletics

As an athletic director at the UA for 30 years, Mary Pavlich Roby brought women's athletics from the basement of the UA athletic forum to perennial contenders in the NCAA.

In 1959 Roby was hired as director of the Women's Recreation Association. Men's and women's intercollegiate programs were combined in 1982 and she became associate director of athletics overseeing 14 of 17 intercollegiate (non-revenue) sports, helping UA's athletic program earn a sixth place overall national ranking.

She played a key role in getting athletic scholarships for women (athletic scholarships for women were nonexistent in the country until 1974). Today women's sports have achieved nearly equal status with men's sports in terms of budgets and support.

"Of course I wish that everyone could enjoy watching a women's tennis match or a gymnastics meet as much as I do, but we have to hope that that will come with time," Roby says.

Dr. Roby has been extremely active in athletic associations over the years, serving as vice president of the Pac-10 Council in 1986 when it first included women's programs.

An Arizona native, she received her bachelor's degree in physical education from the UA in 1948, a master's degree from Smith College in 1949 and a Ph.D. from USC in 1971.

A diehard Wildcat, Roby has also coached at the University of Colorado and at Arizona State University.

Mary Roby. ***Courtesy, University of Arizona Athletic Department.***

changes in national and conference alignments. In 1979, a year after men's sports had moved from the Western Athletic Conference to the Pac-10, the women also turned their eyes westward and, along with Arizona State University, joined five Southern California schools in the Western Collegiate Athletic Association (WCAA). In 1981-82 the AIAW was absorbed by the NCAA and began full slates of women's championships.

In their first year of NCAA competition, UA women's teams would perform quite well, placing sixth nationally in swimming and track and field, eighth in cross country, 13th in golf and 15th in tennis, while three individual titles were won, two in track and field by Meg Ritchie and one by swimmer Diane Johnson.

The national trend was for women's programs to reflect the same conference alignment as their male counterparts, and in 1986-87—after a brief one-year membership in the five-team Pac-10 West Conference—the women's sports teams were welcomed into the Pac-10 fold.

Arizona's most titled woman athlete of the pre-Pac-10 era was Meg Ritchie, a two-time British Olympian and winner of seven AIAW and NCAA titles between 1980 and 1983. She still holds collegiate records in the shot put and discus. Other prominent women athletes of the period were current LPGA standout golfer Chris Johnson, two-time Olympic medalist diver Michele Mitchell, synchro swimming Olympic gold medalists Tracie Ruiz and Candy Costie, and Olympic runner and world champion triathlete Joan Hansen.

NOTABLES

This cartoon poster from the early 1970s shows the member universities of the Western Athletic Conference, of which Arizona was a founder in 1963.

Courtesy, University of Arizona Athletic Department.

When Mary Roby retired as associate athletic director for women in 1989, a new position of associate director of athletics for administrative services was created. In addition to filling the need for a senior woman administrator to represent UA women's programs at the Pac-10 and NCAA level, this position was also given administrative responsibilities for all of these so-called non-revenue sports, both men's and women's. In the 1990s the separation between men's and women's sports was lessened even further when the swimming and diving and track and field programs were each combined under one head coach.

Although UA was a latecomer to the field of women's intercollegiate competition, within the space of just two decades talented and determined

University of Arizona student athletes, inspired coaches and forward-looking administrators have battled unequal funding, inadequate facilities and equipment and lack of respect and recognition to prevail over their opponents both on the field and off.

Exciting teams, such as the 1991 NCAA softball champions, and record-breaking individual performers such as swimmer Crissy Ahmann-Leighton and high jumper Tanya Hughes, who both won NCAA titles and earned U.S. Olympic team berths in 1992, have helped women's sports at the UA become one of the nation's most prominent and successful programs.

Since 1988, when a national publication began its annual all-sport ranking of the top collegiate athletic programs, the UA women have consistently ranked 11th and higher, including fifth-place finishes in 1989 and 1991 and culminating with their highest ranking ever, third, in 1992.

Truly, the lady Wildcats have, like the men, learned to BEAR DOWN.

This 1917 snapshot shows the attire fashionable coeds wore for swimming. This pool still exists today and is situated between the student union and Mines and Metallurgy building. It was covered with a low roof in 1942 and has served since as the UA water reservoir. *Courtesy, University of Arizona Athletic Department.*

he evolution of intercollegiate athletics at the U of A has been and continues to be an exciting and entertaining story, full of characters as gifted and colorful and traditions as rich and meaningful as those of any university in America.

From the very beginning of the university, its student-athletes and coaches have demonstrated a love of competition and an indomitable team spirit. As a result, the university today enjoys a reputation as one of the nation's finest public universities for both academics and athletics.

Now that story, ably written and enhanced by excellent photographs—some never before printed—is more available to our alumni and friends than ever before in this excellent book, BEAR DOWN: The University of Arizona, Intercollegiate Sports—A Photographic Chronicle. *I know you will enjoy it. Bear Down!*

Cedric W. Dempsey
Director of Athletics

Cedric W. Dempsey.
Courtesy, Robert Walker, University Photo Center.

ootball at the University of Arizona can be traced back to the territorial days of 1899, but the game played then bore little resemblance to today's game.

The uniforms and equipment were usually home-made and play was extremely rough with no forward passing and with dangerous formations such as the "flying wedge."

The first football team was organized in January 1899 by Prof. Stewart F. Forbes, brother of university professor Robert H. Forbes, and a former fullback at

TOUCHDOWN!

Football has been played at the University of Arizona for almost 100 years. *Photo: Chris Mooney/ Balfour Walker. Courtesy, University of Arizona Athletic Department.*

Illinois. No games were played until fall when the team was called together again. The first competition was a practice game on November 4 with a Tucson town team, that Arizona won 5-0 (touchdowns counted five points in those days). The first official game was played at Carrillo's Gardens on November 20, 1899, and the same two teams battled to a scoreless tie. The Tempe Normal School provided the first intercollegiate competition, winning 11-2 on November 30. The season ended with Arizona defeating the Tucson Indian team 22-5 in a hard-fought game on January 13, 1900.

Before 1899 there hadn't been much interest in the sport and several tries at forming a team had failed. But in 1899 the students solicited $70 from Tucson businessmen for uniforms and lumber was begged from a local lumberyard for goalposts.

Benito Suarez, a halfback on the 1899 team, recalled how the sport got its start: "We were sitting out in front of South Hall after supper one night," Suarez recalled of campus days in 1899, "when somebody said, 'Let's get up a football team.' We split up, each took a man and started playing. There were a couple of footballs at the school—I don't know where they came from—and some of the boys knew about the sport. Half of us had never heard of football, though.

"When we first started our uniforms consisted of canvas pants and striped jerseys. We took our shoes to town and got a shoemaker to put cleats on them, and for shoulder pads we'd stuff old shirts inside the shoulders of the shirts we played in. There were no programs like calisthenics and drills, but we did get up early and run four or five miles every day. Sometimes we'd run as far as Fort Lowell and back."

The University of Arizona's first football team was formed in 1899. Holding the football is George M. Parker, son of university president Millard M. Parker. Note that the ball is much rounder than the football used today. *Courtesy, Special Collections, University of Arizona Library.*

In 1902 the UA team won all five games, outscoring its opponents 134-0 to claim the territorial title. The previous year the UA manifested a growing spectator interest by installing bleachers along the

field, which at that time was located at the northwest corner of the campus at the site of the present Arizona State Museum.

In 1905 the preps and varsity were separated for the first time and the varsity team played its first out-of-state opponents, traveling to the Los Angeles area, where they were soundly beaten by Pomona College and St. Vincent (now Loyola Marymount) 55-0 in the first night game played on the west coast. No team was fielded in 1906-07, but there was a revival of the sport when the *Arizona Daily Star* offered a trophy to the winner of a best-of-three series between the University of Arizona and the University of New Mexico. The first game was in Albuquerque on Thanksgiving Day in 1908, inaugurating what was to become one of the Southwest's oldest football rivalries.

In 1909 New Mexico evened the series in Tucson, 23-11, and the UA claimed the Stark trophy by default when New Mexico was unable to field a team for the rubber match.

Arizona had had nine different football coaches from 1899 through 1913, none serving for more than two seasons, but things changed radically in 1914 when J. F. "Pop" McKale was hired as the University's first permanent athletic director and coach.

McKale's first two teams were the stuff of legend. The 1914 squad's hard-fought 14-0 loss at Occidental earned the school its nickname of "Wildcats," and the 1915 team's 7-3 upset victory at Pomona inspired students to construct the huge block "A" on Sentinel Peak west of the city that is today's "A" Mountain.

McKale also brought UA football and all other sports into the modern era, upgrading schedules to include top-flight intersectional competition and eventually eliminating non-collegiate opponents. After World War I he had only one losing season and his overall record in 16 seasons was 80-32-6 (.703), including 60-31-6 against collegiate opposition. His 1921 team, which was 7-2 and played then-national power Centre (Kentucky)

College in a post-season bowl game in San Diego, is still ranked as one of the school's greatest grid-iron elevens. His last three squads before stepping down following the 1930 season were a combined 18-3-3 and played games in the L.A. Memorial Coliseum and the Rose Bowl.

In 1931, McKale placed the Wildcat football destiny in the hands of his good friend and associate Fred Enke, head basketball coach and varsity line coach since 1925. McKale remained as director of athletics and continued to coach baseball. Enke was at the helm for one year, managing only a 3-5-1 record. The opening game of the 1931 season was unlike any other since the opening of Arizona Stadium in 1929. The game was played at night on a field brilliantly flooded with 40 single unit reflectors, each burning a 2000-watt lamp. The decision to give night football a trial had been made by the UA Athletic Board of Control because it was becoming impossible for the Wildcats to secure good opponents for early season games at home due to the excessive heat. Unfortunately, the changes in light and temperature didn't help the Wildcat cause, as they were shut out by San Diego State 8-0, suffering their first loss in the new stadium.

In 1932 Enke was replaced as head coach by Lieutenant A. W. ("Gus") Farwick, a former Army All-American R.O.T.C. instructor. His first and only Wildcat team had a 4-5 record. After two years

Coaching Profile: Dick Tomey

The University of Arizona has climbed the ladder of success since Dick Tomey signed on as head coach in January 1987, following 10 successful seasons at Hawaii.

Tomey replaced Larry Smith, who had guided the Wildcats to unprecedented success during his seven years at the helm. Smith, who defected to rival USC, was a tough act to follow. But then Tomey handles heat quite adeptly. Tomey is a part-time firewalker, an unusual hobby he picked up while coaching at Hawaii.

"I've done it a bunch of times," he said. "It makes you realize that you can do something that heretofore would scare you to death. You wouldn't think that you could walk that barefoot, but you can get yourself in a state of mind power—think so that you can do it. It shows how strong the mind is."

That sums up Tomey's philosophy. He believes strongly in "personal development" which includes attending lectures, taking classes and reading a wide range of books.

Tomey is a no-nonsense, get-to-the-point kind of coach, who has found something special in Tucson. "Everyone in the Pac-10 Conference has something which is unique to that place and that program. At Arizona that special something is the spirit," he said. "When you first arrive here, it grabs you. I'm pleased to be involved with that spirit and feeling."

Dick Tomey
Courtesy, University of Arizona Athletic Department.

of losing-football, McKale decided to put the program back on solid footing.

Tex Oliver: 1933-1937

The man who would take Arizona out of the football doldrums and into national respect was Gerald A. "Tex" Oliver. Oliver, who grew up in Texas and played football at Army, earned a Phi Beta Kappa key at USC and had been hired as a temporary track coach by McKale in 1933. McKale asked him to stay on in the fall to take over the football team.

One of his first moves was to begin recruiting players from Southern California, where he had been a highly successful prep school coach. In his first season he quickly revived interest in and support of UA football, going 5-3. In five seasons, his record was 32-11-4, including two Border Conference titles; he'd lost only one game by more than 2 touchdowns, and he had brought UA football into the national spotlight.

Oliver's team not only played well, but they also looked good. They were dubbed the "Blue Brigade" because of their flashy powder blue satin uniforms with bright red piping stripes on their jerseys and pants.

Head coach H.B. Galbraith observes the football team and quarterback Burrell Hatcher in this image dated 1909. No doubt today's coaches would find this formation intriguing. *Courtesy, Special Collections, University of Arizona Library.*

In 1938 Oliver left to take the job at Oregon, whom UA had defeated, 20-6, in the final game of the 1937 season. He was unable to duplicate his UA success at Eugene, going 11-13-2 in three seasons and was quoted many years later as saying: "The worst mistake I ever made was beating Oregon that afternoon."

Orian M. "Toad" Landreth: 1938

To replace Oliver, McKale again went to the Southern California prep coaching ranks, hiring a man with the unlikely name of Orian M. "Toad" Landreth from Long Beach Poly High School. Landreth's first and only season was plagued by squad dissension and untimely injuries to key players. After a disappointing 3-6 record, he was gone.

Miles W. "Mike" Casteel: 1939-1948

After the stormy season under Landreth, McKale looked to the Midwest for his next head coach, hiring Mike Casteel, an assistant at Michigan State.

During Casteel's first three years he took the team to 6-4, 7-2 and 7-3 records. Despite a shortage of players due to military inductions, the 1941 team, led by Little All-American Hank Stanton, who set an NCAA record with 50 catches, tied for the Border Conference title.

In 1943 varsity football was cancelled for the duration of the war. The end of the war in 1945 brought football back to the campus with the Wildcats marking their return by going undefeated and outscoring their opponents 193-12 in an abbreviated 5-game season.

After the war, Casteel was unable to recover his winning touch, posting 4-4-1 and 5-4-1 records in 1946 and 1947, despite the standout play of Arizona's first major college All-American Fred W. Enke, who led the nation in total offense in 1947. In 1948, against the toughest schedule in school history, the Wildcats were 6-4 and were invited to play in the second Salad Bowl at Montgomery Stadium in Phoenix on New Year's Day, losing to Drake, 14-13.

Despite his success, 45-26-3 in eight seasons, Casteel was handed his walking papers following the Salad Bowl. He was replaced that spring by USC assistant and former Trojan All-American Bob Winslow. Ironically, Casteel would go on to become director of athletic fund-raising for arch-rival ASC-Tempe.

QUOTABLES

"I played football at North Phoenix High School but was hurt most of my senior year. I had no intention of playing football in college until I was working out with two Scholarship Freshman Fraternity Brothers from Hawaii and they talked me into going out for spring practice. Thanks to them I received a scholarship that summer and was promoted to linebacker midway through the next fall season (1948)."

Duane D. Miller,
Miller Bros.

Bob Winslow: 1949-1951

While Winslow's teams were not very successful on the field, he did bring a number of firsts to UA football, including the "T" formation,

Orville "Speedy" McPherson was the largest member of Arizona's "little shrimp" backfield in 1914. He went on to become a Tucson civic leader and one of the University's most ardent and supportive alumni. *Courtesy, Special Collections, University of Arizona Library.*

UA-ASU Rivalry Began in 1899

When the University of Arizona and the school now known as Arizona State University first met at Carrillo's Gardens in Tucson, few could have guessed that an enduring rivalry would develop.

ASU, then called the Tempe Normal School, took that first game 11-2, but the next nine contests were played in Tucson—and all were hometown wins.

ASU blitzed Arizona 47-7 in 1957 and 47-0 in 1958 costing UA coach Ed Doherty his job. "They said I could lose every game, so long as we won this," Doherty said.

UA ended a decade of frustration in 1974 by defeating ASU.

The Wildcats won only twice in the next eight years, but the 1980s gave UA a 7-0-1 streak against ASU.

In 1983 Wildcat Chris Brewer twice ran off tackles for first downs on third-down plays in the final two minutes of the game with Arizona trailing 15-14. His runs set up Max Zendejas' winning field goal as time expired for a 17-15 victory.

A fumble on an ASU punt return late in the third period of the 1985 game was recovered by Wildcat Don Be'Ans to cut ASU's lead to 13-10. Two more Zendejas field goals kept ASU out of the Rose Bowl with a 16-15 defeat.

A tackle at the 1-yard line on fourth-and-goal in the 1986 game thwarted a possible Sun Devils comeback, 21-10. The 1987 game ended in a 24-24 tie.

Wildcat victories in 1988, 1989 and 1990 gave the Cats an overall record of 37-26-1 against ASU.

However a nine-game non-losing streak against ASU was finally broken in 1991 when ASU won 37-14 over an injury-decimated UA squad.

A sold-out crowd at a UA – ASU football game. *Photo: Robert Walker. University Photo Center.*

offensive and defensive platooning, the school's first black player, Fred Batiste, the football dorm (discontinued in 1951) and the predecessor of Camp Cochise located at Fort Huachuca.

Winslow's three seasons resulted in a 12-18-1 record as well as academic and police problems. After a humiliating 61-14 drubbing by ASC-Tempe in 1951, Winslow was replaced by Warren Woodson, a highly successful coach for eight years at Hardin-Simmons.

Warren Woodson: 1952-1956

Woodson's teams, featuring the then innovative wing-T formation and standout running backs Ken Cardella and Art Luppino, who led the nation in rushing in 1954 and 1955, was the best since before World War II. Nonetheless, Woodson was gone in January 1957 after evidence of illegal payments to football players and other program irregularities were uncovered.

Arizona was eventually put on one year's probation by the NCAA. Had it not been for the university's self-reporting, the action taken would have been more severe.

Ed Doherty: 1957-1958

Former Boston College All-American Ed Doherty, who had turned the ASC-Tempe program around from 1947-50 and then became an

NFL assistant, replaced Woodson in 1957. With limited resources and the NCAA investigation hanging over his head, Doherty was unable to turn around Arizona's fortunes. The 1957 team posted the worst record in school history and the following season (3-7) wasn't much better, despite the passing combination of Ralph Hunsaker to Dave Hibbert that led the nation with an NCAA record of 61 completions. Following a 47-0 loss to ASC-Tempe, Doherty was gone and replaced by a little-known but highly respected SMU assistant, "Gentleman" Jim LaRue.

After Louis "Slony" Slonaker heads for a huge hole during this 1919 game. The Santa Catalina Mountain Range is in the background. *Courtesy, University of Arizona Athletic Department.*

Jim LaRue: 1959-1966

In 1959 Jim LaRue was handed the job of rebuilding Arizona's grid fortunes and bringing dignity and respect back to the program, tasks that he accomplished with alacrity.

In his first season the team finished 4-6, including a stunning 30-26 upset of Texas Tech, but in 1960 LaRue drove his Wildcats to a remarkable 7-3 season, including six straight victories to end a season highlighted by a drubbing of Arizona State, the UA's first victory over the Sun Devils in five years.

In his third season LaRue took UA to its loftiest heights ever. Led by the "TD Trio" of quarter-

Seven Sensational Plays

1. Larry Smith calls time-out with two seconds remaining and Arizona deadlocked with Notre Dame 13-13 in 1982. The Irish call time-out to make Arizona freshman kicker Max Zendejas "think about" his 48-yard kick. He makes it and the previously undefeated, 8th-ranked Irish and its sellout crowd of 59,065 are silenced.

2. UA is tied with Stanford 27-27 in 1982 with 3:40 remaining when UA quarterback Tom Tunnicliffe catches an 11-yard touchdown pass from tailback Brian Holland as the UA rallies to win 41-27.

3. Jay Dobyns catches an eight-yard pass from Tom Tunnicliffe with 1:01 remaining to give Arizona a 27-24 victory in a nationally televised game against UCLA in 1984.

4. In the 1986 UA-ASU game, ASU trails 24-10 in the fourth quarter but has enough time to rally if it can score from the 8-yard line. UA safety Chuck Cecil intercepts a pass and runs 106 yards for a game-clinching touchdown.

5. A 67-yard catch and run by Jeff Fairholm in 1986 overcomes the Colorado Buffaloes' 21-17 lead with 4:45 remaining for a 24-21 Arizona victory.

6. In 1988 reserve safety Scott Geyer sacks Washington's quarterback with 42 seconds remaining, forcing a fumble on the UW 5-yard line during a 13-13 tie. Gary Coston kicks a 22-yard field goal with five seconds remaining for a 16-13 win.

7. In 1989 undefeated Oklahoma is tied with Arizona 3-3 with two seconds remaining when Doug Pfaff kicks a 40-yard field goal for an upset Wildcat win in Tucson.

back Eddie Wilson and halfbacks Bobby Lee Thompson and "Jack Rabbit" Joe Hernandez, the team was five points away from an undefeated record, posting an 8-1-1 record, the best in 62 years of UA football. The '61 team achieved the school's first-ever top-20 ranking and finished the season tied for 17th in the final AP poll.

LaRue's teams opened the WAC era with 5-5 records in 1962 and 1963, and was 6-3-1 in 1964, claiming a share of the WAC crown, the school's first conference title since 1941.

The team jumped off to a good start in 1965, winning its opener on regional TV at Utah and then upsetting Kansas. But the season went downhill from there with just one more victory to finish 3-7, thus setting off rumblings for LaRue's ouster.

In his final season, LaRue broke from his conservative offense to a wide-open passing game that rewrote all the UA and WAC passing records, but the team finished 3-7 again. Attendance was down and LaRue was out.

Darrell Mudra: 1967-1968

Succeeding LaRue was Darrell Mudra, who held a doctoral degree in education and was considered a miracle worker in small college football. It was hoped that he could work his brand of magic on a UA football program that had only six victories in its last 20 games.

The Notre Dame crowd at South Bend in 1982 was stunned when Max Zendejas' 48-yard, last-second field goal made victors of the Wildcats and losers of the Irish. *Courtesy, University of Arizona Athletic Department.*

During the first year of play under the guidance of Mudra, a powerful Wyoming whipped Arizona in the opener. But then on September 30 Arizona traveled to Ohio State and dealt the Buckeyes a stunning 14-7 defeat, partially due to the brilliance of Bill Lueck. It was the biggest football victory in Arizona history and the highlight of an otherwise disastrous season.

It looked like Arizona's football messiah had finally come when Mudra's second team opened the 1968 season by winning eight of its first nine, its only defeat a narrow 16-13 loss to Big Ten Champ Indiana. The Wildcats were in the hunt for the Sun Bowl, and prior to the season-ending game with Arizona State, Mudra issued an ultimatum to Sun Bowl officials: "Take us now or leave us." The ploy worked; the Sun Bowl named Arizona as one of its two teams. Unfortunately, ASU also had been a contender for the Sun Bowl, and Mudra's maneuver infuriated the Devils. They retaliated with a 30-7 thumping of the Cats, giving Wyoming (whom Arizona had beaten, 14-7) the

GREAT MOMENTS

Cactus Comet Leads Nation in Rushing and Scoring in 1954

Art Luppino
Courtesy, Special Collections, University of Arizona Library.

Art Luppino, the University of Arizona's "Cactus Comet," had one of the most sensational varsity debuts in college football.

In the 1954 season opener, the 5-9, 170-pound sophomore halfback from La Jolla, Calif., carried the ball six times and scored five touchdowns against New Mexico A&M (now New Mexico State). The Wildcats trounced the Aggies 58-0.

Luppino gained 228 net yards in 20 minutes rushing on those six carries. He scored on runs of 37, 48, 74 and 53 yards—and then added another touchdown by returning the second-half kick-off 88 yards.

Despite a predicted defeat for UA when they played the highly regarded University of Utah, UA pulled off a 54-20 upset largely due to the efforts of Art Luppino, who scored on a line plunge, an end run, an off-tackle slant and a 92-yard kick-off return for a total of four touchdowns.

"Kick-off returns were my favorite play," Luppino says. He'd set up the tacklers and go back against the grain. When it appeared he'd get caught, he headed out of bounds.

"I think I originated running out of bounds," he says. "You see it all the time now, but back then fans used to boo me."

Luppino led the nation in rushing two straight seasons (the first player ever to do so), led the nation in scoring and kickoff return yardage and set many UA records, many of which still stand.

Luppino also ran his way right onto the cover of *Parade* magazine, quite a feat for an athlete from what was then considered a small school.

As team after team rigged its defenses to fence him in, Luppino took many a beating on the field. In the 1954 Texas Tech game he was deliberately blind-sided and lost a tooth and received a concussion.

The incident made news nationwide and caused an uproar. Luppino was awarded the Swede Nelson National Sportsmanship Award that season for saying the incident was his own fault. He still maintains he should have been more alert.

Luppino suffered a knee injury in 1956 during the first practice of his senior year:

"It was a dummy scrimmage, no contact intended. But a teammate's hand caught in my shoulder pad and twisted my body around and the knee ripped apart," Luppino says. "I hobbled off and three hours later my foot was bigger than the football."

He says the knee should have been operated on and asked the university to pay for it but was turned down.

He played the 1956 season with limited success. The injury later precluded him from playing pro football and cut short a stint with the minor league Tucson Cowboys.

Luppino returned to UA, took a master's degree, and went back to Southern California where he taught school for 22 years.

Luppino, who was a single wing fullback on his high school team, says he never intended to play football in college. He had an offer from the San Diego Padres baseball team, but a three touchdown summer all-star football game changed his mind.

"I was inundated with offers. You name the school, I could've gone there. Prior to that, only Arizona had shown any interest."

He said his dad lured him to Arizona with the promise of a new car if he stayed until Christmas.

"I was the 18th tailback. In those days, you either made the first 40 or went home," he recalls.

By the third day, Luppino still hadn't touched the ball. He had just about given up on the car. But finally Coach Warren Woodson hollered for the "hot-shot from La Jolla."

Luppino says he did not even know how to get into the proper stance. But he circled end and ran. He raced past the end zone and out onto the track. Coach Woodson grinned.

The "Cactus Comet" played the next consecutive 42 games for Arizona.

Collegiate athletics keep the competitive spirit alive. Gary Cropper played football at the University of Arizona from 1955 through 1959 and is adamant that his athletic adventures have helped shape his successful career. The mental toughness, tenacity and self-confidence he mastered on the UA gridiron are the same attributes that have made Gary Cropper Chevrolet and Chrysler Center in Casa Grande and Cropper's Nogales Auto Center successful enterprises. Cropper learned on the Wildcat football field that "when you are knocked down, you pick yourself up and try again," and says his years at the UA shaped the forthright values and spirit of service found in both of the Cropper auto dealerships.

Gary Cropper
President, Cropper Auto Dealerships

conference title. In the Sun Bowl on December 28, UA played Auburn evenly for a half but finally was overpowered, 34-10.

Soon after the dramatic ending of the 1968 season, UA's Sun Bowl appearance and an 8-2 season that drew record-setting crowds into Arizona Stadium, Mudra resigned. Although he had done what he was hired to do better and faster than anybody dreamed possible, he was unable to overcome his philosophical differences with the UA administration.

QUOTABLES

"In 1946, 1,500 veterans of the World War II, including myself, enrolled in the U of A for the fall semester. We had over 100 men trying out for the football team under head coach Mike Casteel. I now appreciate the intense training, conditioning and drilling our freshmen coaches imposed on us. There were many great coaches and football players, men like Bob Svob, Murl McCain, Joe Peggs, Bob Ruman, John Black and Fred Enke, Sr."

DEL LEWIS,
President/GM/CEO,
KTVK-TV3 Phoenix, Class of '50

Bob Weber: 1969-1972

Because Mudra's coaching staff clearly had some good ideas, UA officials did not want to lose them. At the request of athletic director Dick Clausen, the staff members got together to select someone from their ranks as their personal candidate for the head coaching job. They picked Bob Weber and Clausen concurred.

After three consecutive losing seasons and three straight losses to ASU, Weber got one more chance to produce a winning team in 1972. New UA President John F. Schaefer said: "He deserved a fourth year in which the seniors he recruited as freshmen will be starting players."

After an opening victory over Colorado State, UA was throttled on consecutive weekends by future PAC-10 rivals Oregon, Washington State and UCLA, but rebounded to challenge for the WAC lead, taking a 3-0 league record into Salt Lake City on November 4. In perhaps the most incredible game in UA football annals, the Utes overcame a 27-0 UA lead with 28 points in the fourth quarter. Gone was any hope of a winning season, and gone too was Weber.

It would be up to new athletic director Dave Strack to pick the man to pick up the pieces of UA football and he chose Michigan assistant Jim Young, top aide to Bo Schembechler at Miami and Michigan since 1964.

Jim Young: 1973-1976

Young's first team was nothing short of phenomenal, going 8-3 and tying ASU for the WAC title with a 6-1 league mark, despite a 55-19 loss to the Sun Devils. The team set a school record for total offense, 412.3 yards per game, and Jim Upchurch was the WAC's top rusher with 1,184 yards. Quarterback Bruce Hill and flanker/kick returner Theopolis "T" Bell, both sophomores, emerged as future Wildcat football

Cats Took Aim Against UNM for Kit Carson Game Trophy Rifle

Fifty years ago, the University of Arizona's chief football adversary was not the Tempe Normal School, but the University of New Mexico.

The annual Arizona-New Mexico contest goes back to the territorial days of 1908 and has a history of great games, brilliant individual stars and wonderful anecdotes.

In 1938, UA athletic director McKale and Roy Johnson, chief of New Mexico's sports program, decided that the rivalry warranted recognition and agreed that an old Springfield rifle belonging to McKale would make a good trophy.

The huge, single-shot, bayoneted trophy was named in memory of Indian scout Kit Carson, who had worked in both Arizona and New Mexico.

But McKale let out the story that this was the rifle that had been used to capture Geronimo. Other times he claimed that he had been given the rifle by Kit Carson himself, despite the fact that McKale was born in 1887 and the rifle was manufactured in 1868, the year Carson died.

The Kit Carson Rifle became the object of many memorable gridiron battles during the Border Conference years and throughout the heyday of the Western Athletic Conference in the 1970s. UA's move from the WAC to the Pac-10 in 1978 brought about a near cessation of the football competition with Arizona holding a commanding 41-18-3 edge.

The last time Arizona and New Mexico played was in 1987, when the Wildcats won, 20-9, permanently retiring the trophy which is now on display in the Athletic Development Office-Wildcat Club lobby in McKale Center.

J. F. "Pop" McKale, left, shows New Mexico athletic director Roy Johnson the famous "Kit Carson Rifle." ***Courtesy, University of Arizona Athletic Department.***

Hall of Famers.

Young's second team opened the 1974 season with five straight wins, and following a whopping 41-8 win against the University of Utah, the UA moved into the top ten of the Associated Press collegiate football poll for the first time in the poll's history. The Wildcats got a quick test of their ninth place ranking and lost to Texas Tech, 17-8, at Lubbock, followed by a 37-13 home defeat at the hands of WAC champ BYU, which dashed any bowl game hopes.

The 1974 team finished strong with four straight victories, capped by a 10-0 victory over Arizona State, finally breaking a nine-game losing streak to the Sun Devils. The 9-2 record was a school record for wins. Young duplicated it the following season, missing out on the WAC title and a Fiesta Bowl bid when ASU edged the Cats 24-21 on "the catch" by John Jefferson. Following a disappointing 5-6 mark in 1976, Young resigned to take the head coaching job at Purdue. Approaching membership in the much tougher Pac-10, Strack opted for a coach with previous head coaching experience: Tony Mason, a former Michigan and

Following their 15-13 victory over longtime rival New Mexico in 1977, jubilant UA football players celebrated with the winners' trophy, the Kit Carson Rifle. All-America defensive lineman Jon Abbott is number 93. Following that season Arizona left the WAC for the Pac-10 and would not meet the Lobos again for ten years. (Note the "moving A" on the helmet.) *Photo: Jack Schaefer. Courtesy, University of Arizona Athletic Department.*

23
93

GREAT MOMENTS

Comeback Cats of 1961 Were Murder On Faint-Hearted Fans

Football program, 1961. ***Courtesy, University of Arizona Athletic Department.***

It was a team of superlatives.

Arizona closed its 1960 football season with a brilliant march of six straight victories and thereby set up its 1961 team for a chance at an all time school record. In 1961 the Wildcats were predicted to have the best season in 25 years. They did.

In all the history of Arizona football the 1961 team was the poorest game starter and the greatest finisher. It was the team that turned the fans to ice in the first quarter then sizzled them into roaring loyalty with great and dramatic fourth-quarter finishes.

One such great victory was the 1961 20-15 triumph of the Wildcats over Wyoming with only a minute and 32 seconds to play. Although that spectacular finish set off a fist fight on the field, and even left one of the officials reeling and bleeding slightly, it was just one in a long line of successful heart-stoppers that season.

The 1961 Wildcats featured a constellation of backfield stars like quarterback Eddie Wilson (third-team All-American), center Bob Garis and Bobby Lee Thompson and Joe Hernandez (all honorable mention) and won the University of Arizona a national grid ranking for the first time in its history.

The 1961 schedule was demanding, and still the Cats battled Nebraska of the Big Eight to a 14-14 deadlock, and upset Oregon (15-6), Wyoming (20-15) and ASU (22-13)—in all four cases battling from behind late in the game much to the delight of a contingent of frenzied fans that will long remember them as the "Comeback Cats."

When Jim LaRue took over the Arizona football program in 1958 it was no honor to be a member of the squad. The coeds looked more longingly at the tennis letter sweaters than at the members of an oft-beaten football team. Three seasons later there was chest-swelling over an 8-1-1 season, including the all-important victorious smacking of Arizona State.

In 1961 a pair of fleet-footed halfbacks were running and scoring at the fastest pace in five years. Jackrabbit Joe Hernandez, the long-legged right halfback with an uncanny knack of catching key passes, was teamed with bouncing Bobby Lee ("The General") Thompson, UA's left halfback with the jet propelled start. Dubbed the "Touchdown Twins," once they got the ball, Hernandez and Thompson brought crowds to their feet with jet-like speed on tackle slants as well as end sweeps.

Eddie Wilson guided the Wildcats to their all time best football record in the fall of 1961 with his cool, second-half direction of the team that turned certain defeats into victories.

With the exception of Colorado State University, Oregon and the Hardin-Simmons University games, all of Arizona's opponents got the jump on the 1961 Wildcats. Only twice did UA fail to rebound into the victory column—in the 14-14 tie with Nebraska and in the 27-23 upset loss to West Texas State.

In each instance it was the calm handling and radar-accurate passing of Wilson that brought the Wildcats back to victory.

In Portland, Oregon, Wilson passed and punted the University of Oregon into submission as Arizona produced a 15-6 upset, getting all its points in the second half.

After Hernandez scored his third touchdown in the waning moments of the game, Wilson hit Thompson with a two-point conversion pass that gave Arizona a 22-21 verdict over upset-minded New Mexico.

And then against previously unbeaten Wyoming, Wilson hit Thompson with a 33-yard touchdown pass with only 1:32 left in the game to give UA a 20-15 victory.

Finally, with Arizona trailing 13-10 at halftime in its battle with archrival ASU, Wilson blasted the Sun Devil defense in the second half to pace the 22-13 triumph. He hit Walt Mince with a 31-yard touchdown pass and scored the go-ahead touchdown with a five-yard run. When the goalposts came tumbling down, Wilson had completed 9 of 19 passes for 116 yards.

Both Wilson and Thompson were second round draft choices of the National Football League's Detroit Lions. Walt Mince was drafted by the Los Angeles Rams.

In 1961, one of the UA's finest football seasons was reflected by a 16th-place ranking in the Associated Press' next-to-last poll of the season. Coach Jim LaRue's Wildcats, owners of an 8-1-1 record, moved up from 20th place after their 22-13 victory over ASU.

The 1961 Wildcat football team personified the nickname columnist Bill Henry gave Arizona back in 1914—"the fighting wildcats."

The 1961 Wildcat football team was a top-notch bunch of boys and a favorite of the fans. They were dubbed the "Comeback Cats" due to their propensity for dramatic fourth-quarter finishes, and ended the season with an 8-1-1 record, the best in 25 years. The Westward Look Resort is also a first-class establishment and has had many loyal guests during its 45 years of distinguished service in the hospitality industry. Spread over 80 acres of beautifully landscaped grounds overlooking Tucson, Westward Look Resort is the recipient of AAA's 4-Diamond Rating, the Travel/Holiday Award for Fine Dining, and Tennis magazine's "Top 50" award.

Purdue assistant, who had turned Cincinnati from a 2-9 loser to a 9-2 winner in 1976.

TONY MASON: 1977-1979

Despite getting the Wildcats into the 1979 Fiesta Bowl, where they lost 16-10 to Pittsburgh, Mason's overall record of 16-18-1 was not impressive and the revelation of serious recruiting and financial aid violations during his tenure led to his downfall.

LARRY SMITH: 1980-1986

Larry Smith had been Jim Young's defensive coach at Arizona, and then went on to turn Tulane from a losing program to a 9-3 team in 1979. When he took over from Mason, the threat of adverse NCAA action seemed imminent, but it was three agonizing years before the sanctions were levied.

Smith's first Wildcat team in 1980 probably overachieved to post a 5-6 mark, but it pulled off one of the greatest upsets in school history with a 23-17 victory over No. 2-ranked UCLA, behind the heroics of freshman quarterback Tom Tunnicliffe.

Smith got the program back in the winning mode in 1981, shocking USC in Los Angeles 13-10, and was 6-4-1 the following season. The 1982 team also began the UA's nine-year gridiron domination of in-state rival Arizona State, knocking the Devils out of the Rose Bowl.

On May 20, 1983, the NCAA placed the Arizona football team on three years' probation: no bowls for 1983-84 and no TV games in 1984-85. The sanctions were for 18 violations committed from 1971-79 in connection with recruitment and payments to players.

QUOTABLES

"John S. Collins attended the college of Civil Engineering from 1954 to 1958. He was a perfect blend of scholar and sports fan. He graduated "with distinction" in 1958 and enjoyed almost every game his alma mater participated in until his death from cancer in 1979. One of the last football home games he attended found him sitting in a downpour, cheering for his beloved team, and having a temporary getaway from his medical treatment."

JERRY A. COLLINS,
Collins-Pina Consulting Engineers, Inc.

Despite the NCAA penalties, Smith persevered, opening the 1983 season with four straight wins and achieving the school's highest ranking: 2nd by *Sports Illustrated* and 3rd by AP and *USA Today*. That 1983 team, led by the school's first consensus All-American linebacker Ricky Hunley, went 7-3-1 and the following year the Cats were 7-4.

Smith led his teams to records of 8-3-1 in 1985 and 9-3 in 1986, tying Georgia 13-13 in the 1985 Sun Bowl and defeating North Carolina 30-21 in the 1986 Aloha Bowl—the UA's first ever post-season victory. The 1986 team was ranked 10th in the final UPI poll and 11th by the AP.

UA GRIDDERS PLAY IN EIGHT BOWL GAMES

Bowl fever has hit Tucson on eight occasions during the past 70 years.

1921 East-West Christmas Classic. Centre 38, Arizona 0. San Diego, Calif.—Centre College of Kentucky splashed to a rainy 38-0 victory.

1949 Salad Bowl. Drake 14, Arizona 13. Phoenix, Ariz.—Two fumbles, an interception and a missed extra-point attempt kept UA from a tie.

1968 Sun Bowl. Auburn 34, Arizona 10. El Paso, Tex.—The Tigers scored 24 points to crush the Wildcats 34-10.

1979 Fiesta Bowl. Pittsburgh 16, Arizona 10. Tempe, Ariz.—The Pittsburgh Panthers survived a late rally to win.

1985 Sun Bowl. Arizona 13, Georgia 13. El Paso, Tex.—Both teams returned kickoffs and made field goals to tie the match.

1986 Aloha Bowl. Arizona 30, North Carolina 21. Honolulu, Hawaii—Arizona capitalized on big defensive plays to win its first ever postseason victory.

1989 Copper Bowl. Arizona 17, North Carolina State 10. Tucson, Ariz.—Arizona took the lead in the first half and held off a threatening Pack in the second to give coach Dick Tomey his first bowl victory.

"Wildcats" celebrate their Copper Bowl victory. *Photo: Chris Mooney/Balfour Walker.*

1990 Aloha Bowl. Syracuse 28, Arizona 0. Honolulu, Hawaii—The shutout snapped Arizona's 214-game scoring streak, the second longest scoring streak in NCAA history.

Following the 1986 season, Larry Smith shocked and disappointed his Tucson supporters when he left to take the top job at Pac-10 rival Southern California.

Dick Tomey: 1987-Present

Named to succeed Smith was Hawaii mentor Dick Tomey, who had first been considered for the UA job when Young left in 1976. Tomey introduced an innovative, hybrid offense utilizing wishbone and run-and-shoot principles with mixed success.

Despite inconsistency with the new offense, which came to be known as the "wish-and-shoot," Tomey's first team was better than its unusual 4-4-3 record. Two of those ties and two losses were against the Pac-10's top four teams, all of whom went to bowl games.

Safety Chuck Cecil, who had destroyed ASU in 1986 with his 106-yard interception return seen on national TV, bolstered his selection as the UA's second consensus All-American with a school and Pac-10 record four interceptions against Stanford. He finished as the conference's all-time pass pick-off leader with 21.

Dick Tomey was "fit to be tied" considering the three deadlocks, two of which were the result of missed placekicks, and frustrating losses of 15-14 to Iowa in the season opener and 12-10 at USC, in a game in which the Trojans failed to score a touch-

The marching band makes halftime memorable at UA football games. *Photo: Chris Mooney/Balfour Walker.*

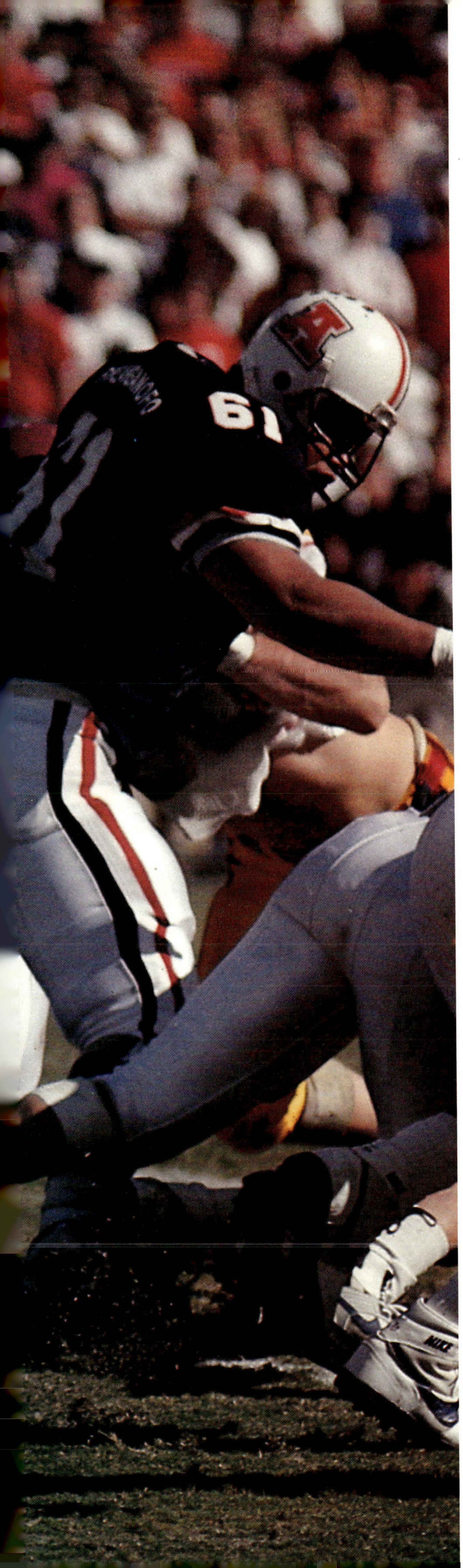

down. The unbelievable final seconds of the UA-ASU game in Tempe that resulted in a 24-24 tie seemed a fitting end to an unusual season.

Vance Johnson (#25), famed for his football exploits, as an All Pac-10 running back, achieved his greatest renown with his winning leap at the 1982 NCAA track and field championships. *Photo: Mike Stoklos. Courtesy, University of Arizona Athletic Department.*

Left: *Sports Illustrated* rated Arizona Stadium's turf the best in America. *Photo: Balfour Walker.*

Over: School spirit sets UA football apart from the rest. *Photo: Edward McCain.*

A mid-season slump in which the Cats dropped three of four games in Arizona Stadium cost Tomey's 1988 team, which finished strong with three straight victories to go 7-4, but missed out on a bowl bid it surely deserved. The biggest win was a 16-13 victory in rainy Seattle, the UA's first over Washington in six tries since joining the Pac-10.

In 1989 the Wildcats posted victories over national powers Oklahoma, UCLA and Washington in posting an 8-4 record, which included a 17-14 victory over North Carolina State in the inaugural Copper Bowl in Tucson. The 1990 season was one of ups and downs on the way to a 7-5 record and a 28-0 mauling by Syracuse in the

Cats
Cats

Aloha Bowl. The loss, in Tomey's first return to Honolulu, was the UA's first shutout since 1970, ending a 214-game consecutive scoring streak that was the nation's second longest.

The inconsistent 1990 Wildcats defeated three bowl teams and became only the second team in 75 years to beat both UCLA and USC in Los Angeles. But they also lost to lowly Oregon State and suffered their worst Pac-10 defeat ever at the hands of Washington, 54-10. The star of the team was cornerback Darryll Lewis, who won the Jim Thorpe Trophy as the nation's outstanding defensive back and became the UA's third consensus All-American.

A plague of injuries to key players ended any hopes of a winning record in 1991. Despite the emergence of freshman Chuck Levy as a star of the future, the 4-7 record was UA's first losing season in 10 years and a 37-14 loss at ASU ended a nine-game winning streak against the Sun Devils. Most UA supporters are convinced that 1991 was an aberration and that Tomey has what it takes to put the Wildcats back on the winning road.

An epidemic of injuries in the 1991 season pressed multi-talented freshman Chuck Levy into service at quarterback, his fourth position. Fittingly, he was named First Team All Pac-10 all-purpose back. *Photo: Scott Borden. Courtesy, University Photo Center.*

Right: Fullback Mike Streidnig (#33) takes the ball against the Pacific Tigers in 1989. *Photo: Chris Mooney/ Balfour Walker.*

33

University of Arizona Football Statistical Highlights

Seasons' Records

		Collegiate			Non-collegiate		
Year	Coach	W-L-T	PF	PA	W-L-T	PF	P4
1899	Stewart F. Forbes	0-1-0	2	11	1-0-1	22	5
1990	William Skinner	0-0-0	0	0	3-1-0	131	6
1901	William Skinner	0-0-0	0	0	4-1-0	115	17
1902	Leslie Gillett	1-0-0	12	0	4-0-0	122	0
1903	(None)	No varsity football					
1904	Orin 1. Kates	0-0-0	0	0	3-1-2	64	48
1905	Wm.. M. Ruthrauf	0-2-0	5	96	5-0-0	113	0
1906	(None)	No varsity football					
1907	(None)	No varsity football					
1908	H.B. Galbraith	1-0-0	10	5	4-0-0	126	0
1909	H.B. Galbraith	1-1-0	17	23	2-0-0	54	0
1910	George F. Shipp	2-0-0	19	2	3-0-0	68	6
1912	Ray L. Quigley	1-1-0	36	30	1-0-0	19	0
1913	F.A. King	1-2-0	13	42	1-0-0	13	0
1914	J.F. "Pop" McKale	3-1-0	51	20	1-0-0	21	0
1915	J.F. "Pop" McKale	2-3-0	14	34	3-0-0	119	O
1916	J.F. "Pop" McKale	2-3-0	147	93	3-0-0	100	0
1917	J.F. "Pop" McKale	2-1-0	67	38	1-1-0	41	3
1918	(None)	No football, World War I					
1919	J.F. "Pop" McKale	5-1-0	173	19	2-0-0	80	0
1920	J.F. "Pop" McKale	4-1-0	163	45	2-0-0	218	20
1921	J.F. "Pop" McKale	4-2-0@	149	55	3-0-0	269	1
1922	J.F. "Pop" McKale	5-3-0	90	53	1-0-0	19	0
1923	J.F. "Pop" McKale	3-3-0	79	114	2-0-0	67	13
1924	J.F. "Pop" McKale	2-4-0	40	93	0-0-0	0	0
1925	J.F. "Pop" McKale	3-3-1	70	88	0-0-0	0	0
1926	J.F. "Pop" McKale	4-1-1	89	18	1-0-0	54	0
1927	J.F. "Pop" McKale	3-2-1	100	59	1-0-0	63	0
1928	J.F. "Pop" McKale	5-1-2	152	110	0-0-0	0	0
1929	J.F. "Pop" McKale	7-1-0	182	22	0-0-0	0	0
1930	J.F. "Pop" McKale	6-1-1	122	33	0-0-0	0	0
					Conference#		
					W-L-T	Pl.	
1931	Fred A. Enke	3-5-1	72	149	1-1-1	2	
1932	A.W. "Gus" Farwick	4-5-0	82	106	3-2-0	2	
1933	G.A. "Tex" Oliver	5-3-0	113	35	3-2-0	3	
1934	G.A. "Tex" Oliver	7-2-1	138	54	2-1-1	3	
1935	G.A. "Tex" Oliver	7-2-1	218	45	4-0-0	1	
1936	G.A. "Tex" Oliver	5-2-3	190	54	3-0-1	1	
1937	G.A. "Tex" Oliver	8-2-0	194	88	3-1-0	3	
1938	Orian M. Landreth	3-6-0	75	146	0-3-0	5	
1939	Miles W. Casteel	6-4-0	109	113	1-2-0	4	
1940	Miles W. Casteel	7-2-0	204	83	3-1-0	2	
1941	Miles W. Casteel	7-3-0	253	146	5-0-0	1T	
1942	Miles W. Casteel	6-4-0*	189	139	4-2-0	4	
1943	(None)	No football, World War II					
1944	(None)	No football, World War II					
1945	Miles W. Casteel	5-0-0*	163	12	(No conference play)		
1946	Miles W. Casteel	4-4-2	218	136	2-2-1	4	
1947	Miles W. Casteel	5-4-1	233	Z41	3-2-0	4	
1948	Miles W. Casteel	6-5-0@	167	246	3-2-0	3T	
1949	Robert E. Winslow	2-7-1	118	298	2-4-0	6	
1950	Robert E. Winslow	4-6-0	214	257	2-4-0	6	
1951	Robert E. Winslow	6-5-0	246	270	4-3-0	4	
1952	Warren Woodson	6-4-0	285	155	3-2-0	3	
1953	Warren Woodson	4-5-1	234	161	3-1-0	4	
1954	Warren Woodson	7-3-0	385	215	3-2-0	4	
1955	Warren Woodson	5-4-1	184	169	1-2-1	5	
1956	Warren Woodson	4-6-0	120	182	1-3-0	5	

University of Arizona Football Statistical Highlights

Year	Coach	Collegiate W-L-T	PF	PA	Conference# W-L-T	Pl.
1957	Edward A. Doherty	1-8-1	125	297	0-4-0	6
1958	Edward A. Doherty	3-7-0	83	276	2-1-0	**
1959	Jim LaRue	4-6-0	118	211	1-2-0	**
1960	Jim LaRue	7-3-0	233	152	3-0-0	**
1961	Jim LaRue	8-1-1	288	131		
1962	Jim LaRue	5-5-0	134	171	2-2-0	2
1963	Jim LaRue	5-5-0	136	165	2-2-0	2
1964	Jim LaRue	6-3-1	147	76	3-1-0	1T
1965	Jim LaRue	3-7-0	77	172	1-4-0	6
1966	Jim LaRue	3-7-0	192	250	1-4-0	5
1967	Darrell Mudra	3-6-1	162	231	1-4-0	5
1968	Darrell Mudra	8-3-0@	186	149	5-1-0	2T
1969	Robert W. Weber	3-7-0	210	276	3-3-0	5
1970	Robert W. Weber	4-6-0	168	213	2-4-0	5
1971	Robert W. Weber	5-6-0	191	232	3-3-0	3
1972	Robert W. Weber	4-7-0	226	271	4-3-0	4
1973	James C. Young	8-3-0	295	219	6-1-0	1T
1974	James C. Young	9-2-0	264	174	6-1-0	2
1975	James C. Young	9-2-0	330	169	5-2-0	2
1976	James C. Young	5-6-0	283	273	3-4-0	5T
1977	Tony Mason	5-7-0	256	250	3-4-0	5T
1978	Tony Mason	5-6-0	245	205	3-4-0	6T
1979	Tony Mason	6-5-1@	244	243	4-3-0	3T
1980	Larry Smith	5-6-0	215	275	3-4-0	6T
1981	Larry Smith	6-5-0	253	205	4-4-0	6T
1982	Larry Smith	6-4-1	311	219	4-3-1	5
1983	Larry Smith	7-3-1	353	118	4-3-1	5
1984	Larry Smith	7-4-0	272	192	5-2-0	3T
1985	Larry Smith	8-3-1	252	146	5-2-0	2T
1986	Larry Smith	9-3-0@	352	204	5-3-0	4T
1987	Dick Tomey	4-4-3	263	220	2-3-3	7
1988	Dick Tomey	7-4-0	179	171	5-3-0	3T
1989	Dick Tomey	8-4-0@	248	178	5-3-0	2T
1990	Dick Tomey	7-5-0@	267	311	5-4-0	5
1991	Dick Tomey	4-7-0	248	361	3-5-0	6T

@-Includes bowl game

** Total includes one non-collegiate game*

#-Border Conference, 1931-60; Western Athletic Conference, 1962-77; Pacific 10 Conference, 1978-present

*** Did not play enough games to qualify for title*

Arizona's Bowl Game Record

Date	Bowl Game Site	Opponent	Score
12-26-21	Christmas Classic, San Diego	Centre (Ky.)	0-38
1-1-49	Salad Bowl Phoenix	Drake	13-14
12-28-68	Sun Bowl, El Paso	Auburn	10-34
12-25-79	Fiesta Bowl, Tempe	Pittsburgh	10-16
12-28-85	Sun Bowl, El Paso	Georgia	13-13
12-27-86	Aloha Bowl, Honolulu	North Carolina	30-21
12-31-89	Copper Bowl, Tucson	North Carolina St.	17-10
12-25-90	Aloha Bowl, Honolulu	Syracuse	0-28

Career Top Ten

Scoring		(TD-PAT-FG)
360*	Max Zendejas, 1982-85	(0-123-79)
337	Art Luppino, 1953-56	(48-49-0)
246	Lee Pistor, 1974-75	(0-120-24)
203*	Gary Coston, 89	(0-83-40)
194	Vance Johnson, 1981-84	(32-1-0)
190	"T" Bell, 1972-75	(31-2-0)
146	Ken Cardella, 1951-53	(24-2-0)
128*	Hubie Oliver, 1977-80	(21-1-0)
124	Bobby Thompson, 1961-62	(20-2-0)
120	Charlie McKee, 1969-71	(20-0-0)

** 2 Pt. Extra Point*

Season Top Ten

Scoring		(TD-PAT-FG)
166	Art Luppino, 1954	(24-20-0)
99	Max Zendejas, 1983	(0-39-20)
97	Gary Coston, 1986	(0-34-21)
96	Art Luppino, 1955	(13-18-0)
89	Max Zendejas, 1985	(0-23-22)
86	Max Zendejas, 1984	(0-23-21)
82	Bobby Thompson, 1961	(13-3-0)
80	Lee Pistor, 1975	(0-35-15)
79	Max Zendejas, 1982	(0-37-14)
78	Vance Johnson, 1983	(13-0-0)

Game Top Ten

Points Scored		(TD-PAT-FG)
32	Art Luppino vs. NM St., 1954	(5-2-0)
25	Art Luppino vs. Utah, 1954	(4-1-0)
24	Ronald Veal vs. Wash. St., 1935	(4-0-0)
24	Richard Hersey vs. Pacific, 1980	(4-0-0)
24	Harry Holt vs. UTEP, 1970	(4-0-0)
24	Don Beasley vs. Ariz. St. 1953	(4-0-0)
23	Art Luppino vs. W. Tex. St., 1954	(3-5-0)
22	Art Luppino vs. Idaho, 1954	(3-4-0)
21	Art Luppino vs. New Mex., 1954	(3-3-0)
20	Art Luppino vs. W. Tex. St., 1955	(3-2-0)
20	Charles Beall vs. San Diego St., 1945	(3-2-0)

LOYOLA
24
00
20

asketball, which was invented in 1891, had a start of sorts at the University of Arizona in the fall of 1897 when at least one game was played between chosen teams, the final score being 3-1.

In 1898, a few students collected enough money to purchase a basketball. They played on a dirt court in front of the Mines Building and the ball was of such poor quality that it lasted only one game.

The situation improved dramatically in 1903 when construction began on the

Anthony "A. C." Cook, preeminent Wildcat blocker, doing what he does best in a game against Loyola. *Photo: Chris Mooney/Balfour Walker.*

SHOOTING FOR THE TOP

school's first gymnasium, Herring Hall. The first basketball games were played there during the 1903-04 school year. The first team to play outside competition was formed in 1904-05 and was coached by Orin Albert Kates, who was also the school's athletic director. It defeated the Morenci YMCA 40-32 and tied the Bisbee YMCA 19-19.

The university claimed the territorial championship, winning two of three from the Bisbee YMCA.

Charles E. Woodell, a member of the 1903-06 university teams, recalled in a 1950 interview with the *Wildcat:*

"We were not allowed to dribble and could only use one pivot foot. Any rolling ball in those days was free. Fouls were called for the same infractions as today."

Under various coaches, no more than five games were played in any season, principally against YMCAs and Tucson High School, until 1913-14, when nine games were played, including the first collegiate contests. The "U," coached by Raymond L. Quigley, beat the Tempe Normal School 41-17 and 15-10 and split a pair of games with the Gila Academy, which later became Eastern Arizona Junior College.

J. F. McKale took over coaching the basketball team in 1914 and coached through the end of the 1920-21 season, posting a 49-12 record, although just 18 victories were over collegiate teams.

Asa Porter, seated on the floor,and his teammates posed with coach J. F. McKale in a 1915 basketball team photo. Note the players' pants, which were carry-overs from football. *Courtesy, Special Collections, University of Arizona Library.*

In 1917 the UA made its first barnstorming tour, playing six games in three states—Arizona, New Mexico and Texas—in six days, including New Mexico and New Mexico State.

Two of McKale's court stars were men who later became prominent UA leaders. A. L. Slonaker became Dean of Men and the first executive secretary of the Arizona Alumni Association from 1922-40. His teammate, Bill Pistor, became head of Animal Pathology.

Basketball was played a little differently in those days. Slonaker once commented on the biggest changes in the game since his time: "For one thing, the idea of a center jump after every basket has been discontinued. This old rule slowed down the game considerably."

The other change was the lack of substitutions. "In those days," Slonaker said, "mass substitutions were unheard of. Five men often played the whole game."

Bill Pistor remembered the equipment: "We had to furnish most of our own equipment. We had one basketball and Coach McKale used to take it home every night to recondition it for the next day's play."

The cumbersome uniforms of the early 1920s featured long bloomer-like pants with long sleeved shirts. "We boldly broke the bloomer pants tradition in my last year," Pistor said, "when we donned short pants."

The 1920 Wildcat basketball team, including "Slony" Slonaker, third from right, lined up for a photo beside Old Main. By this time, the team had acquired basketball shorts. As basketball was McKale's least favorite sport, he gave up his coaching position in 1921. *Courtesy, University of Arizona Athletic Department.*

Limited seating and hazardous playing conditions in the close quarters of Herring Hall forced the Wildcat cagers off campus in the early 1920s, with most games being played at Tucson High School or the National Guard Armory until the new men's gymnasium (soon to be called Bear Down Gym) was completed for the 1926-27 season.

Schedules began to be upgraded and non-collegiate opponents became infrequent. James H. Pierce, who replaced McKale as head coach in 1921-22, played a four-game home-and-home series with Southern California, winning one game each in Tucson and in Los Angeles. The following year Pierce's squad, led by the UA's first true bas-

ketball star, Harold Tovrea, won 17 of 20 games, including six of eight from UCLA and USC.

Tovrea was a prolific scorer in an era when few teams averaged more than 40 points a game. In 1922-23 he scored 316 points, nearly half the team total of 679, averaging 15.8 per game. The following season he averaged 17.3 (294 points in 17 games) and set a school single-game scoring record of 35 points against New Mexico Mines that would last 31 years. His career total of 805 points (with stats unavailable for three of the 55 games he played) was the UA record for nearly a quarter of a century.

With the hardest schedule ever attempted (including USC and California) the 1924 Arizona team record was 14-3, an excellent record compiled against 13 teams of collegiate standing. The UA beat every Arizona, New Mexico and Texas team they played and captured the Southwest Championship. In addition, they split with the Pacific Coast champions, California. The Wildcats scored an average of 40.5 points per game, for a total of 689 points, while holding their opponents to only 352.

An exceptional recruiter, teacher and tactician, Lute Olson is recognized as one of the best "bench" coaches in the game. Olson's assumption of UA's coaching reins in 1983 signalled an abrupt turnaround of the bottomed-out UA program and the beginning of the next era of Wildcat basketball greatness. *Photo: Edward McCain.*

Fred Enke: 1925-1961

The modern era of Arizona basketball began with the hiring of Fred Enke as head

LUTE OLSON MOLDS ARIZONA INTO A SOLID WINNER

LUTE OLSON.
Photo: Robert Walker. Courtesy, University Photo Center.

Lute Olson came to Arizona from Iowa and took the Basket Cats from the bottom of the heap to the top of the elite. Likewise, Jim H. Houtz, chairman, chief executive officer and founder of CyCare Systems, guided his company from a small firm located in Dubuque, Iowa, to one of America's leading providers of information management systems and services to the medical group practice. CyCare also made a move to Arizona, and the company's headquarters are now in Phoenix. Just as Coach Olson provides the Wildcats with courtside solutions, the healthcare industry depends upon CyCare to provide answers to business management problems.

JIM H. HOUTZ
Chairman, CEO and founder, CyCare Systems

Dapper and handsome, Lute Olson looks more like a TV evangelist than the head coach of the UA basketball team. Yet, few are better at what he does.

Olson took a program with a 4-14 season in 1983 and in five years went to the Final Four with 35-3.

He's not called "Cool Hand Lute" for nothing. You won't see him jumping up and down on the sidelines or throwing a chair across the court. He has a calm approach to the game.

"I just don't think a team can be under control if the coach isn't," the soft-spoken Olson says.

Tucson has been wild about the Cats since Olson took over. In 1983 the Cats sold about 5,000 season tickets and averaged little more than 6,000 fans at home games. Now, season ticket sales have soared and the average home attendance for regular season games is a Pac-10 record of 13,636 a game.

Steve Kerr, who played for Olson and then graduated to the NBA, remembers standing across the street from the basketball arena and unsuccessfully trying to give tickets away.

"He (Olson) spent his first few years telling everybody to get their tickets because, in a couple of years, they'd be gone," says Kerr. "He was right."

Olson took the Cats from the bottom of the heap to three straight perfect home records: 14-0 in 1990, 14-0 in 1989 and 19-0 in 1988, the nation's longest home-court winning streak of 47 games.

Under Olson, the Wildcats have been Pac-10 league champions in 1986, 1988, 1989 and 1990, gone to the Final Four in 1988, and made the NCAA Sweet 16 in 1989.

"It's important to build a *program*, rather than build a team," he stresses. "You'll see some schools that have a good team one year and, all of a sudden, you don't hear about them for a few more years.

"I think that was the strength of the program at Iowa, too. We had a really good team in '79, when we first went to the playoffs, and lost some key people. And yet, the next year we were in the Final Four . . . We've sustained it, and that's the same thing I've tried to do in building the program at Arizona."

Tried? Olson's 214-76 UA record speaks for itself.

Olson was a three-sport athlete and star at Augsburg College (Minn.) from 1953 to 1956 and after five years of prep coaching in Minnesota, he coached for seven years in California.

He guided Long Beach City College to three league titles and the 1971 state junior college crown. He was 24-2 in one season at Long Beach State before guiding Iowa to a successful nine-year run.

He left Iowa with eight years remaining on a 10-year contract, a huge home that was among his perks, a lucrative radio-TV package and one of the richest basketball camps in the nation.

But after nine years at Iowa, Olson, a family man, was ready for a milder climate and the excellent facilities at Arizona.

Olson's players have been very impressive on the hardcourts, classrooms and in the community. They're out and about in Tucson, warning against drug use and raising money for medical causes.

Lute Olson is not simply winning basketball battles. He's a winner on all fronts.

coach in 1925-26 and the beginning of play in Bear Down Gym in 1926-27. And what a beginning it was!

Enke, a former All-Big Ten football and basketball player at Minnesota, had coached football and basketball at South Dakota and had been basketball coach and athletic director at Louisville before being hired by McKale. He won the first of his 11 Border Conference titles in 1932-33, but it was in the years following World War II that Enke-coached squads brought the University its greatest-ever prominence in collegiate athletics.

In the six seasons from 1945-46 through 1950-51, the "Enkemen" won 75 percent of their games (132-45), captured six straight Border Conference crowns with an overall league record of 82-15 (.845) and appeared in post-season tournaments or playoffs six times. Arizona played in the National Invitational Tournament (NIT) in Madison Square Garden in 1946, 1950 and 1951, in NCAA district playoffs in 1948 and 1949 and at the NCAA Championship in 1951. And from 1945-51 Arizona won an incredible 81 straight home games without a loss.

QUOTABLES

"In the early 1950s, Bear Down Gym was very small. When Phi Gamma Delta had Bill Kemmeries on the varsity basketball team, it was a must to go to home games. If you didn't get there early, there were no seats, so an advance party always got there early.
Great then—great now!"

JOHN S. MUELLER,
CEO,
Laidlaw Corporation

Enke's great 1950-51 squad, led by the unrelated Johnson & Johnson duo of Roger, the school's first basketball All American, and Leo, who is still the UA's single-season total rebound leader, ranks among the finest in school history. Another star of that squad was Leon Blevins, who set a new all-time Wildcat scoring mark when he tallied a season total of 452. Blevins was famous for high scoring from all angles of the court and was drafted by the professional Indianapolis Olympians.

This team posted a 24-6 record (15-1 in the Border Conference), including a victory over defending NCAA/NIT champion CCNY, and was ranked 12th nationally in the final Associated Press poll, its highest national ranking. Earning berths in both the NIT and NCAA tournaments, which was permitted in those days, Arizona lost in the first round to eventual tourney runners-up, Dayton (NIT) and then dropped a thriller to Kansas State (59-61) in the second round at the NCAA playoffs.

Arizona's 62-61 upset of fourth-ranked Long Island University before an overflow crowd of 4,600 (nearly a thousand over its listed capacity of 3,600) at Bear Down Gym on January 29 still ranks as one of the most celebrated victories by any Wildcat team in any sport.

Enke had built a national powerhouse almost exclusively with Arizona high school players, but his inability (or reluctance) to vigorously recruit out-of-state talent took its toll during the 1950s, and he would record only one winning record (14-13 and a Border Conference co-title in 1952-53) in his final 10 seasons, the low point an embarrassing 4-22 mark in 1958-59.

Although Enke's final 10 seasons were mostly forgettable from a wins and losses point of view, a number of memorable players trod the hardwoods of Bear Down Gym during the 1950s. Among them was the school's first black player Hadie Redd in 1951-52; gunner Bill Kemmeries, whose 32 field goal attempts against Hardin-Simmons in 1952 is still the most ever by a Wildcat cager; Eli "Teddy" Lazovich, who scored a school-record 38 points in a memorable 104-103 overtime loss to ASU in 1955; smooth Ed "Pudge" Nymeyer, the second UA player to score 1,000-plus points in three seasons (1,225); rugged board-pounder Bill Reeves, who still holds the UA's best single-season rebounding average of 13.2 per game in 1955-56; and the unstoppable Ernie McCray, who rewrote the the UA hoop record book from 1958-60. The slim 6' 5" former Tucson High star scored 1,349 career points, and in a banner senior season averaged 23.9 points and 12.2 rebounds per game. He also set the still-standing single-game scoring record of 46 against Los Angeles State.

> QUOTABLES
>
> "Carl's Jr. of Tucson is proud to be a Wildcat sponsor for the UA basketball team. Being new to Tucson, it has been a thrill to see the spirit and support this city gives UA and its athletes. We certainly enjoy the games and look forward to a great Wildcat tradition of winning and its tradition of excellence."
>
> FRANK KARCHER,
> *Owner,*
> *Carl's Jr. of Tucson*

By the beginning of the end of the Border Conference era, both Enke and Bear Down Gym were beginning to show their age. In 1959 former Wildcat player and highly successful junior college coach Bruce Larson was hired as Enke's first full-time assistant and heir apparent.

The "Grand Old Man" of Arizona basketball finally retired following the 1960-61 season, ending a 38-year career as head coach, a total that still ranks eighth all time in NCAA annals. At the time of his retirement he was one of just five college mentors to have won 500 games, finishing with 525 career victo-

Bill Reeves (#42), "the man who never saw overtime" is firmly camped in the UA basketball record book. In the 1956-57 season, Reeves led the nation by averaging 4.3 fouls per game and fouling out of 13 contests, both statistics still UA records. However, Reeves also ranks as one of UA's greatest rebounders: his 26 boards against UCSB in 1956 and per-game average of 13.2 in 1955-56 are school records as well. Also pounding the boards are Bill Wagner (#53) at left and Bob Mueller at right. *Courtesy, University of Arizona Athletic Department.*

ARIZONA
53
42
TECH
57

Fred Enke: The Grand Old Man of Arizona Basketball

Fred Enke coached at UA for 38 years and had an outstanding 510-326 career. After his college career as an All-Big Ten football and basketball player at the University of Minnesota, he coached basketball at the University of Louisville.

In 1925, J. F. "Pop" McKale asked his friend, Notre Dame's Knute Rockne, for names of possible basketball coaches for Arizona. Rockne gave him only one—Fred Enke.

In 1943 UA posted a 22-2 record. In 1946 they were invited to the NIT at Madison Square Garden, losing to Kentucky, the eventual champion.

His most sensational season was during his silver jubilee year, 1950-51, Enke's 25th as head coach. Doublemint gum and an old tan sport coat spiritually guided him through that season. "I guess I'm superstitious," Enke suggested. But his players knew Enke was color blind and his tan sport coat matched everything.

That season UA upset City College of New York 41-38 as well as number-one Long Island University 62-61, finished the season 24-6 and played in the NIT and the NCAA tournaments.

Enke's resignation also ended the "coaching career" of Charlene Enke, who for years had helped with the personal problems of the players. "It's been a most gratifying and wonderful experience, all these years together in coaching," she said when he retired.

Fred Enke ushered in the modern era of UA basketball. *Courtesy, University of Arizona Athletic Department.*

ries, 510-326 at Arizona.

Although hundreds of players would come and go and nearly 1,000 games would be played, for 36 years the name Fred Enke and Arizona basketball would be synonymous. Even today one of the most enduring records of Arizona basketball history is the 81-home-game winning streak, the fifth longest in NCAA history, that Enke fashioned in Bear Down Gym from 1945 through 1952.

Enke's overall mark for 35 seasons in Bear Down's cozy confines was 297-85, a dominating .777 winning percentage, and included only one season with a losing home record. [Note: Enke's successor, Bruce Larson, was 101-34 (.748) in Bear Down and also had only one losing record there in 11 seasons. Fred Snowden won all seven of the games his team played there in 1972-73 before moving to McKale Center for the final five games of the season.]

The final UA varsity game in Bear Down Gym was played on January 18, 1973, a 79-77 victory over UC-Santa Barbara that brought Arizona's overall record there in 47 seasons to an impressive 405-119 (.793).

Bruce Larson: 1961-1972

Bruce Larson had played for Fred Enke two seasons on the old coach's great teams of the late 1940s and after graduating in 1950 had gone on to become one of the brightest young coaching prospects in the business. He first took Eastern Arizona to the national junior college tournament championship game, and then Weber JC (which is now Weber State) of Utah to consecutive JUCO finals, winning the national title in 1959.

Larson quickly got the UA program turned around and made it competitive in the new and much more challenging Western Athletic Conference, which included traditionally strong teams such as Utah and Brigham Young and emerging national powers New Mexico and Arizona State. Within three years he had produced the school's first round-ball winner in 11 years, posting a 15-11 mark in 1963-64.

The 1964-65 team (17-9) was probably Larson's best team. Led by classy point guard Warren Rustand, who was an Academic All-American and student body president, and jumping jack forward Albert Johnson, it had a mid-season streak in which it won 10 of 11 games, posted victories over top 10 teams BYU and San Francisco, and achieved its first national ranking (14th in the UPI poll following the 71-56 victory over 8th-ranked USF) since the Enke glory days.

The following year the Cats finished 15-11, with three of the losses coming in overtime, one to eventual NCAA champion UTEP (then known as Texas Western) on the Miners' home court. They were in the running for the WAC title until the final week of the season. But with the exception of a 17-10 record in 1968-69 (a pair of one-point losses to Wyoming costing the Wildcats their first WAC title), Larson was not able to field a winning team in his final six seasons.

Construction on the long awaited new basketball arena, McKale Center, had finally gotten underway in the fall of 1970, and in 1971-72 it was decided to try to improve upon flagging attendance at Bear Down Gym by playing all nonconference home games at the Tucson Community Center. Larson's team missed the cozy confines of Bear Down, and the home court advantage was the reason conference games were still played in the antiquated structure. Bear Down was figured to be worth about 10 points a game to the Wildcats. Of the seven games played at the new downtown facility, the Wildcats lost five on their way to a

QUOTABLES

"My last game was against New Mexico and an Albuquerque paper ran a story about the wild star with the glass eye (I had lost an eye in a childhood accident) who was a leading scorer. That night I scored 24 points. With two minutes left, the coach took me out to a standing ovation. A sportswriter called out, 'Udall, you're a liar. No one shoots like that with a glass eye.' I plucked out the slippery orb and gave it to him, saying, 'Mister, I haven't been able to see much out of this one, you try it.'"

MORRIS K. UDALL,
Former U. S. Congressman, 2nd District of Arizona

G R E A T M O M E N T S

Udall Brothers Hit the Hardwoods for UA

Brothers Stewart L. Udall and Morris K. Udall came to the University of Arizona from St. John's, a city in northeastern Arizona which at that time reputedly had a basketball backboard in every yard. They worked for their room and board, were outstanding students and class leaders, and were standout basketball players.

Stewart Udall, who later went into politics and served as Secretary of the Interior under the late President Kennedy and was also in the Johnson administration, had a split basketball career. He played for the Wildcats as a guard in the 1939-40 and 1940-41 seasons and then was called to military duty during World War II.

An adept guard, Stewart was an All-Border Conference selection in the 1939-40 season. And even then the team leader was a politician—he once led a petition drive to get the UA to play better opponents.

Stewart Udall
Courtesy, Special Collections, University of Arizona Library.

Stewart returned to star for Arizona's 1946 basketball team which won the Border Conference championship and was the first UA team invited to play in the National

disastrous 6-20 record and a last place finish in the WAC. Afterward Larson's tenure as UA cage boss ended, with just four winning seasons in 11 years, and an overall record of 136-148.

Captain Harold Tovrea

To fill the new McKale Center arena and quickly upgrade the level of Arizona basketball, new athletic director Dave Strack would take a bold and courageous step.

Harold "Tove" Tovrea averaged 17.3 points per game in 1923-24, a UA record for a quarter century and the second best until 1960. Against New Mexico Tech he scored 35 points, a school record for more than three decades and still the 10th best in UA history. Scoring almost 45% of the team's points, he led the Wildcats to a 43-8 overall record and 8-4 against UCLA and USC.
Courtesy, Special Collections, University of Arizona Library.

Fred Snowden: 1972-1982

The man Strack chose to take Arizona into the college basketball big time was Fred ("The Fox") Snowden, a former Detroit high school coaching legend who had been an assistant for four years under Johnny Orr, Strack's successor as associate athletic director at Michigan.

Incidental to his coaching credentials, but of major significance at the time, was the fact that

Invitational Tournament in New York's Madison Square Garden, falling to Kentucky 77-53.

Mo Udall, who had a legendary 30-year career as a representative from Arizona's second Congressional District and also gave Jimmy Carter a run for the Democratic nomination for President, lettered for the UA in basketball in the 1942 season. He was called to military duty and returned following World War II.

Mo became a standout performer for Arizona in the 1947-48 season, winning first team All Border Conference honors. After graduation, he went on to play for a year on the Denver Nuggets expansion club.

Mo got his chance to play in 1947 under odd circumstances. He was riding the bench until one night when a starter, sulking because he had been put on the sidelines, was slow in reporting when Coach Fred Enke called him to go into the game. Noting the lackadaisical attitude of the player, Enke looked down the bench and waved at Mo. "Go ahead in at center," Enke told Mo.

Mo went from a bench-rider to a first-string forward on that 1947 championship Wildcat basketball team by sinking 11 points in the closing five minutes of a narrow win over West Texas State.

Mo had to overcome an almost insurmountable handicap for a basketball player. Due to a childhood accident he lost an eye—and his depth perception. Nonetheless, he was school president as well as high scorer in an important Arizona-New Mexico game.

The 1947-48 team on which Mo Udall starred had a 19-10 record and was Arizona's first representative in the NCAA championship postseason playoffs. In the tournament held at Dallas, the Wildcats lost to Baylor, 64-54.

In 1966 both Stewart Udall and Morris Udall were among a select group of congressmen and Cabinet members honored by the NCAA in Washington, D.C. for distinguishing themselves "academically and athletically during their undergraduate years."

That day in the nation's Capitol, Stewart Udall was asked to respond to the honors in behalf of all the Cabinet members. He said: "Looking back from where I am now it is not so far off to the college campus as you might think. Collegiate athletics keep the competitive spirit alive, and this is the essence of American society. They talk about character building in athletics jokingly. It is not a joke at all."

Arizona's Stewart Udall and Morris K. Udall are two outstanding examples of how athletics can build character and how the leaders of today have often been formed on the athletic fields of yesteryear.

Morris Udall
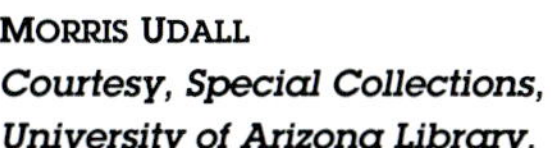
Courtesy, Special Collections, University of Arizona Library.

Snowden was the first black man to be hired as head coach of a major sport (i.e., football or basketball) at an NCAA Division I university.

Snowden did a first-rate public relations job of selling himself, his players and his enthusiasm for Arizona's basketball future to the community. And he wasted no time backing up his bravado with immediate results.

In just three seasons he had the UA in postseason play and in his fourth year he was just one game away from a Final Four berth. McKale Center, which opened on February 1, 1973, with 13,652 fans on hand to see the Cats top Wyoming 87-69, was regularly packed to the rafters with supportive fans, averaging 12,995 per game for the five games played there that season.

In Snowden's first five years, the Wildcats were nearly invincible in McKale, winning 95 percent of their games (62-3). At one point they won 38 straight and it would be eight years before a UA team would lose two in a row at home.

Snowden's first team, featuring a starting lineup of four freshmen which became known as the "Kiddie Korps," went 16-10 overall and 9-5 in the WAC, one game shy—a 110-105 overtime loss to Arizona State in McKale—of winning the

ARIZONA
00
UCLA
42

school's first league title since 1953. Forward Coniel Norman broke Ernie McCray's school scoring record, averaging 24.0 points per game, becoming the first freshman to be named first-team All-WAC. Frosh guard Eric Money averaged 18.9 to earn second-team all-league honors, as Snowden's racehorse offense shot a school record .482 from the field, averaging 81.2 points per game.

Despite the return of the nucleus of the "Kiddie Korps," and the addition of blue-chip frosh Bob Elliott and Herman "Herm the Germ" Harris, who would go on to sensational UA cage careers, Snowden would have to wait until the 1975-76 season to claim his first WAC title. Norman and Money left school for the NBA "hardship" draft following the 1973-74 season.

The 1974-75 team, led by Elliott, a first team All-WAC pick as a sophomore, and junior Al Fleming (along with guard Jim Rappis one of two remaining "Kiddie Korps" alumni), would become the first UA team to make a post-season appearance in a quarter century. With NCAA berths still limited to just 32 teams, the 1974-75 Wildcats were picked to play in the short-lived National Commissioners Invitational Tournament (NCIT), in Louisville, Kentucky. They defeated East Carolina and Purdue to reach the championship game, where they lost to Drake, 83-76.

QUOTABLES

"I remember the first time my dad took me to a U of A basketball game. I was about 12 years old and I was awed by how incredibly large Bear Down Gym seemed. I became a true red-and-blue U of A sports fan from that day forward. While the arenas have gotten bigger and better, nothing quite compares to the magic I experienced on my first visit to old Bear Down."

STEVE RUSSO,
Cox & Russo, P. C.

Snowden's UA basketball revival would finally reach fruition in 1975-76 as the Cats, behind the scoring and rebounding of Elliott and Fleming, and the exciting floor play of Rappis and Harris, would sweep to their first WAC title with an 11-3 league mark, a No. 12 ranking in the final UPI national poll and their first NCAA berth since 1951.

Arizona defeated Georgetown 83-76 in first round NCAA play at Tempe to advance to the West Regionals at Pauley Pavilion. In one of the most exciting games in school history, the Wildcats upset third-ranked and 29-1 Nevada-Las Vegas 114-109 in overtime to earn the right to play defending champion UCLA for a berth in the Final Four. Snowden's charges battled the home-standing, heavily favored Bruins on even terms for most of the game before finally succumbing, 82-66.

Twice All Pac-10, Anthony Cook was Arizona's dominant big man of the 1980s. "A.C." finished up in 1989 as the premier shot blocker in Arizona history and one of the leading career rebounders. Here, in a 1989 Wildcat victory over UCLA in McKale Center, Cook stuffs in two points as the Bruins' Don MacLean looks on helplessly. *Photo: Edward McCain. Courtesy, Edward McCain.*

GREAT MOMENTS

Steve Kerr Excelled Against All Odds

Steve Kerr.
Photo: Tom Bingham. Courtesy, University of Arizona Athletic Department.

The old joke was that when long-suffering fans would call McKale Center and ask, "What time does the game start?" the answer would be, "What time can you be here?"

For years when the Wildcats were bad, they were very bad. And when they were good, well, they seldom were. That changed in 1983 with the arrival of Head Coach Lute Olson, direct from seven winning seasons at the University of Iowa, and Steve Kerr, a freshman from Pacific Palisades, California, who had been recruited by virtually nobody except Olson.

During the 1987-88 season, of course, the Wildcats had more than a flirting acquaintance with a national No. 1 ranking and chalked up wins over such powerhouses as Syracuse, Michigan and Duke. The Cats also made their first appearance in the Final Four.

Much of the credit went to 6'3" Steve Kerr, a fifth-year senior who was also a point guard extraordinaire who sank 60 percent of his three-point shot attempts per game.

Steve Kerr wasn't the most talented Wildcat, but he was the gutsiest—hitting the floor for loose balls with a reckless disregard for elbows and knees.

Says Coach Olson: "Steve was the glue that held that team together. He had an unbelievable awareness and leadership on the court."

Nicknamed "Opie" by his teammates because of his boyish Mayberry R.F.D. looks, Kerr had been considered by scouts too small to play forward and too slow to make up for his lack of size. But when Coach Olson saw Kerr playing in a summer league in Los Angeles, he saw a kid with court savvy that more than made up for his shortcomings.

As a freshman, he played sixth man and an important part of a resurgent program. Then on January 18, 1984, Kerr was awakened by a phone call from his minister. His father had been assassinated. Malcom Kerr was president of the American University in Beirut, where two gunmen reputedly from the Islamic Jihad shot him as he stepped off a campus elevator. Two days after his father's death, Kerr played in Arizona's game with arch rival ASU.

"It was what my father would have wanted. It would have been horrible not to play," Kerr says. "I didn't feel like it was some courageous decision."

Before the game, the packed house stood for a minute of silence in honor of Dr. Kerr. As he took his place on the bench, Steve broke into tears.

It was on that night that the special relationship between Kerr and the Tucson fans was forged. Within seven minutes, the kid with the scruffy blonde hair came off the bench and immediately swished a jumper from almost 25 feet, a shot out of his normal range that year.

Kerr scored 12 points, one of his highs that freshman year, and Arizona's 71-49 win ended a nine-game losing streak to the Sun Devils.

Kerr's travails weren't over. Playing for the U.S. team in the 1986 World Championships in Madrid, a primer for the Olympics, he blew out the ligaments in his right knee, going up for a jump shot. He sat out his senior season and underwent nine excruciating months of rehabilitation. The next season, his last at Arizona, he came back quicker and stronger than before.

Steve Kerr is aware his story is unique, but he isn't looking for a sympathy vote.

"I don't like it when people say I had bad breaks while at Arizona," he says. "I've been one of the luckiest people in the world. The knee injury taught me tenacity. And my father's death helped me put things in perspective."

After a stint with the Phoenix Suns, Kerr is now playing for the Cleveland Cavaliers. He credits his success to the UA basketball program.

"I improved my game 200 percent while playing for Coach Olson," Kerr says.

Steve Kerr walked on at Arizona with no special talent and walked off with the heart of the whole city of Tucson.

Steve Kerr's selection as an All-American and the nation's most courageous athlete in his senior year were ample evidence of his value as a team player to the UA basketball program. Similarly, since its founding in 1943, Tucson Medical Center has emphasized the importance of teamwork in patient treatment and recovery. Today, Tucson Medical Center's 2,385 employees adhere to that tradition, combining teamwork with the most up-to-date technology to provide the highest quality patient care available.

Donald G. Shropshire
President and CEO, Tucson Medical Center

Finishing 24-6, Arizona basketball was back in the national spotlight, but unfortunately not for long.

The following year the Wildcats would fall one game short of defending their WAC title, and lose in the NCAA first round to Southern Illinois 91-77 to finish 21-6. It was Snowden's third consecutive 20-win season, a first at the UA. Elliott concluded his brilliant career as the UA and WAC career scoring leader with 2,131 points, was named a Helms Foundation All-American and was a three-time Academic All-American.

For whatever reason, the coach who had been the winningest coach in the WAC in his first five seasons—102-39 overall and 48-22 in the league—was unable to maintain his magic touch. As the UA prepared to move up to the Pacific-10 Conference, it was apparent that the hounds were catching up with "The Fox."

Dramatic back-to-back victories over USC and UCLA at McKale and a 16-11 record in the first season (1978-79) of Pac-10 play temporarily revived flagging support. But then followed three consecutive losing seasons, during which attendance dropped by more than 3,000 per game. For Snowden, the writing was on the wall, and on January 8, 1982, just before the Pac-10 season opener against Washington, he announced his resignation.

The final ledger on Snowden's ten years at the helm would show an overall record of 167-108 (.607) and 54-30 in the WAC (.643) and 114-29 (.797) in McKale Center. Unfortunately, most of those wins came in his first five seasons, while nearly two-thirds of the losses came in the final five. In his four years in the Pac-10, his record was just 50-58 overall and 28-44 in conference games.

It was hard to believe that "The Fox" would end his career with a 9-18 record, barely better than the 6-20 mark that had preceded his arrival in 1972.

QUOTABLES

"In 1952-1953 I was on the basketball team, the Border Conference champs. Heading into a game in Flagstaff against the Lumberjacks of Arizona State College, now Northern Arizona University, Coach Enke gave one of his famous pre-game talks. He said, 'Okay, men, we're up here in hostile Lumberjack territory. Let's show 'em that our five-game winning streak is not mere *happenstance*!' We all looked at each other, and Bill Kemmeries, our captain, pipes up, 'Happenstance?!?' And Enke says, 'Well, let's just go out and get 'em.' We won by something like 30 points. The game had 90 fouls in it, 50 on us—all but five guys fouled out. It's still an NCAA record."

DR. BILL SMITHERAN,
Professor and Counselor,
Long Beach (California) City College

BEN LINDSEY: 1982-1983

It is unfortunate that the last major official act as athletic director by Dave Strack—whose overall contributions to the development of intercollegiate athletics in his 10-plus years at the UA cannot be overestimated—was his decision regarding Snowden's successor.

In all fairness, the dour Lindsey brought

GREAT MOMENTS

Sean Elliott Breaks Pac-10 Career Basketball Scoring Record

Photo: Edward McCain.

February 18, 1989. Sean Elliott, the University of Arizona's first team All-America forward, stood at the free throw line in McKale Center. A capacity crowd of 13,641 spectators was on its feet as Elliott approached the Pac-10 career scoring record of 2,325 points held by former UCLA center Lew Alcindor, known later as Kareem Abdul-Jabbar.

Everyone was waiting for the 20-year-old record to fall. They knew the 6'8" senior was the man to bring it down. They were right.

Elliott, who was born and raised not 10 miles from where he made the free throw, tied the career record on a layup with 8:48 left for a 77-44 lead. Then, after missing an 18-foot jumper a moment later, he broke the mark with the first of two free throws.

That point, scored with 7:10 left in the Arizona-UCLA game, gave Elliott the Pacific-10 Conference basketball scoring record with 2,326 points. He made the next free throw and left the game.

It was a big game for Sean Elliott, but a nightmare for the Bruins who took a 102-64 drubbing—the worst defeat in school history. They came to McKale to play a basketball game, but instead became a subplot to a momentous event.

A day before the historic game, Kareem Abdul-Jabbar told a *Tucson Citizen* sportswriter that he didn't remember setting the Pac-10 basketball career scoring record. He wasn't even aware that he had it and claimed to have no idea it was about to be broken.

But Sean Elliott knew the record was about to become his—even though 34 points separated him from the milestone as the opening tip went up.

By the end of the first half, he had made seven of 11 field goals for 20 points—nearly half of UA's 41 points—with four assists and six rebounds.

As he approached the mark, the message board flashed the countdown to Elliott, five points to go. Then it was three. Then it was one. Then it was gone.

Sean Elliott set his record in 123 games in four seasons. Lew Alcindor scored 2325 points in 90 games over three seasons. The former UA forward says the discrepancy doesn't bother him.

"I don't care if they put an asterisk by my name or not. It's still the top one on the list," says Elliott.

Alcindor set the Pac-10 scoring record from 1966 to 1969. Freshmen have only been eligible to play at the Division I level since 1972.

During the 1987-88 season, Sean Elliott led the Cats to the Final Four with a 19.6 average. After scoring 743 points—the most scored in one season by a Wildcat and 23 percent of the team scoring—he knew it was possible to get the 506 points he needed to break the record.

But capturing the career scoring record didn't happen quite the way Elliott had envisioned it. He had wanted to clinch the scoring title with a bit more style.

"I had a fantasy that I would drive down the lane and stuff the ball," he says.

But finally Elliott began to feel it didn't matter how the points came. He attempted two three-pointers that would have broken the record. As the ball rolled around the rim on both potential baskets, Elliott was practically begging the ball to go in. It didn't either time.

"Those shots were just teasing me," Elliott recalls.

The crowd was on its feet and held its collective breath during each of Elliott's possessions. Then when he drove toward the basket, with the message board reading, "One more point," Bruin Trevor Wilson fouled him.

From the bench the Wildcats broke into a spontaneous ovation of Elliott as he set up for the shot. He smiled—everyone knew that the Pac-10 career basketball scoring record was to be his.

Elliott had already exceeded Lew Alcindor's free throw total of 699 (Elliott had 703), and Elliott had made the most free throws in conference history (549). Former Oregon State center Mel Counts had held that record for 25 years at 543.

When Sean Elliott made Pac-10 history, Tucson took pride in its home town hero. His achievement was added to the growing list of success stories the community points to with pride.

Intergroup Healthcare Corporation is also on the list. In just over 10 years, Intergroup has grown from a good idea into one of the nation's leading managed healthcare companies, providing health care benefits to approximately a quarter million Arizonans.

Rick Barrett, president and CEO of the Tucson-based company, is a Tucson native and a major supporter of the University of Arizona, including programs such as the Health Management Resource Institute, Children's Research Center and the UA athletic program.

with him decent credentials, having won two NAIA national titles in 16 years at tiny Grand Canyon College in Phoenix. Hired on March 31, less than a month after the end of the 1981-82 season, he had less than two weeks to complete recruiting and, frankly, didn't inherit much talent from Snowden's final squad.

Not a great deal was expected of Lindsey's first UA team, but not even the most pessimistic anticipated the disaster that would befall Arizona basketball in 1982-83. The 4-24 record was the worst in the 79-year history of the sport at the school and is still the poorest by a league team in the 14 years of the Pac-10's existence. The 1-17 conference mark is also a conference low (equaled by Washington State in 1989-90). Lindsey's mild Cats lost eight straight home games, the most ever by a UA team, and were the only team in school history not to win a single away game, going 0-15 on the road.

The season was beset with rumors of off-court shenanigans by Lindsey and his staff, reports of Lindsey's inadequate knowledge of coaching theory and basketball techniques, disorganized practices, lack of supervision during road trips and squad disharmony, which resulted in one player quitting at midseason and five others saying they would not return if he were rehired. By the time Lindsey had begun his first practice in the fall of 1982, the University had a new president, Dr. Henry Koffler, and a new athletic director, Dr. Cedric Dempsey, who had replaced Strack in September 1982. As soon as the calamity of the 1982-83 season was over, these two doctors decided to administer strong medicine to restore the health of the UA basketball program.

NOTABLES

The most efficiently unselfish player in UA basketball history is guard Russell Brown, whose career-assist total of 810 is almost 400 more than the second-place total.

Courtesy, University of Arizona Athletic Department.

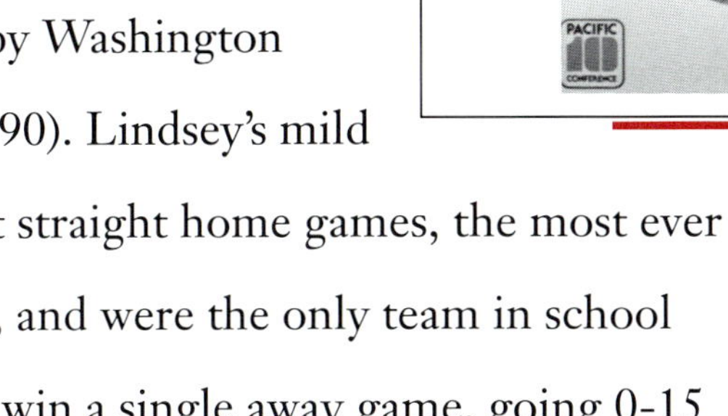

Lindsey was promptly fired, although a suit in which he claimed that he had received verbal assurance that he would be given sufficient time to build a winning team would drag on for several years, eventually ending up in a settlement in civil court.

LUTE OLSON: 1982-PRESENT

Whatever the legal distractions pertaining to Lindsey's firing, Dempsey just wanted to get on with the university basketball program and restore it to a position of national respect and competitiveness in the Pac-10. First of all, he had to find a

Like the 1987-88 Basket Cats, University Medical Center has set a standard of excellence. UMC is a place of trials and explorations — of hope and of life. Above all, it is a place of unsurpassed accomplishments. The hospital strives for excellence in patient care while remaining a research and education facility. One of UMC's most important tasks is to anticipate and meet the state's health-care challenges. The three-fold mission of University Medical Center is indispensable because of today's complicated illnesses, high-tech equipment, and the search for knowledge that remains at the forefront of medicine.

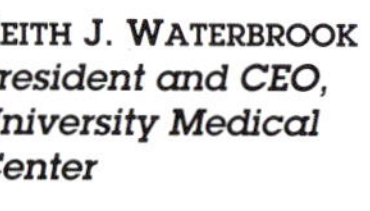

KEITH J. WATERBROOK
President and CEO, University Medical Center

UA Basket Cats Take First Trip to NCAA Final Four

In each college basketball season there's one place where the rainbow ends—at the Final Four.

Only one team comes away with the pot of gold. The 1987-1988 Basket Cats were within reach but only caught a glimmer of the treasure that is the NCAA Championship.

There will never be another season quite so special because there is no other time like the first time. Any subsequent trip to the Final Four that follows for the University of Arizona just won't carry the same thrill.

The 1987-1988 Basket Cats set the lasting example by which excellence is measured. The five starters—three seniors and two juniors—relied on their experience and talent to take the UA to the Final Four.

It wasn't just the number of victories that season that was impressive; it was the quality. Arizona had five victories over Top 10 teams and two more over teams in the Top 20. Of those seven, only two wins were at home.

The opponents were formidable, but Arizona barely flinched when it was asked to face the best. They fell in this order: No. 3 Syracuse; No. 9 Michigan; No. 3 Iowa; No. 5 Duke; No. 7 North Carolina. Iowa was a victim again in the NCAA playoffs. North Carolina was the last hurdle before the Wildcats reached the Final Four.

The winning qualities of the Wildcats went virtually unnoticed until their first public display against the Soviet Union National Team, regarded as the world's best ama-

replacement. His search began at the NCAA Midwest Regional in Kansas City where he and Koffler were sizing up both Iowa's Lute Olson and Villanova's Rollie Massimino as their teams played each other in Kemper Arena.

When Villanova won 55-54, Dempsey immediately obtained Iowa's permission to approach Olson and two days later the hiring of Olson was announced.

Despite being double- and triple-teamed during much of his three varsity seasons at Arizona (1957-60), Ernie McCray broke every Arizona scoring record and became the first Wildcat to score 1,000 points in a career. Today, McCray still ranks in Arizona's top ten in 15 offensive categories and holds the UA record for points in a single game: 46. *Courtesy, University of Arizona Athletic Department.*

"I'm not sure we'd have been able to attract him or if I'd have been able to wait much longer if he'd made it to the Final Four," Dempsey says.

Olson had taken Iowa to the Final Four in 1980 where he was named National Coach of the Year, but his failure to do

teur basketball team. Arizona manhandled the Soviets at McKale Center, winning by ten points.

The 1987-1988 season began with four glorious days in the north that culminated in Arizona's first trip to the Final Four. Anticipation grew when the Wildcats headed for the Great Alaska Shootout, where two favorites—Syracuse and Michigan—were expected to meet for the title. But a UA uprising put a fresh face among the powers of college basketball when the Wildcats left Alaska with the Shootout championship and victories over the two powerhouses. The Wildcats beat Michigan 79-64, and followed with an 80-69 victory over Syracuse in the championship.

The Wildcats were ranked No. 1 in the nation by The Associated Press for the first time in school history.

They clinched their Pac-10 title in Los Angeles at famed Pauley Pavilion and also won first and second round games against Cornell and Seton Hall in the NCAA tournament there.

Next, Arizona earned its trip to the Final Four with victories over Iowa and North Carolina at Seattle's Kingdome.

The championship slipped away on a dreary night in Kansas City. The 86-78 loss to Oklahoma was heartbreaking, but the achievements of the season cast their long shadow over the pain. The memories drowned out the disappointment, and the players held their heads high as they returned to a resounding celebration at Arizona Stadium, where 20,000 fans welcomed their Wildcats home.

Photo: Robert Walker. University Photo Center.

so in 1983 would prove to be a godsend for Arizona basketball.

Olson immediately started rebuilding with two talented junior college transfers, Pete Williams and Eddie Smith, and a lightly recruited freshman guard named Steve Kerr to bolster the dispirited remnants of the Ben Lindsey disaster. His first team was 11-17, winning six of its last eight games and recording the school's first Pac-10 first division finish (tied for fifth) in five years.

Bob Elliott was one of the greatest players in UA basketball history. All Conference, All America and Academic All America, "Big Bird" rewrote most of the UA record book during his 1974-77 career. A decade later his records were broken by another Elliott: Sean. In 1986-87 Bob Elliott served as president of the Arizona Alumni Association. *Courtesy, University of Arizona Athletic Department.*

Kerr's inspired 12-point performance off the bench in a 71-49 victory over Arizona State on January 20, 1984, just days after his father, Malcolm, had been assassinated by Arab terrorists in Beirut is probably the most emo-

tional moment in Arizona basketball history.

The following year the Wildcats were 21-10 and tied for third in the Pac-10 at 12-6, just one game behind co-champions Washington and USC. And they were in post-season play for the first time since 1977, losing to Alabama 51-40, at the NCAA Midwest First Round in Albuquerque.

That would begin a streak of eight straight NCAA Championship appearances, highlighted by the Final Four in 1987-88, five Pac-10 titles and 20 or more wins in seven of nine seasons. In the last five seasons under Olson, the Wildcats have been in the national rankings for 82 consecutive ranking periods. After achieving their first number one ranking in December 1987, Olson teams have been top-ranked 11 different weeks, and at one point, were in the top 10 for 56 straight weeks.

Olson's first major recruiting coup was the school's first "Parade" All-American, Craig McMillan, in his second season, followed the next year by local prep phenom Sean Elliott from Cholla High in Tucson. Elliott would go on to break Lew Alcindor (Kareem Abdul Jabbar)'s Pac-10 career scoring record and earn national Player of the Year honors in 1988. He, Kerr, McMillan, Anthony Cook and transfer Tom Tolbert made up the nucleus of Olson's greatest Arizona team, the Final Four squad of 1987-88, that was ranked number one for six weeks and finished with an incredible 35-3 mark.

Kerr and Elliott were also key members of the 1986 U.S. World Championship team, coached by Olson, which until the 1992 U.S. Olympic "Dream Team," was the only American national team to win a major international championship since the 1984 Olympics.

Since Olson arrived on the scene, the Wildcats have dominated the Pac-10, winning more than 75 percent of their league games (123-39) and winning the conference post-season tournament three straight years before the event was discontinued in 1990. Over the past five seasons, Arizona, bolstered by back-to-back 17-1 seasons in 1988 and 1989, has posted a winning mark of nearly 85 percent against Pac-10 teams.

One of the most remarkable accomplishments of the Lute Olson era was the 71-game con-

QUOTABLES

"As co-captain of the 1954-1955 Wildcat basketball team, I have many recollections of 'bearing down,' but the most remarkable athletic performance occurred in 1951 at the Arizona – New Mexico football game when Allan J. Stanton, converted from defensive end (where he played the week before) to quarterback and led the Wildcats to a 35-20 win. All Stanton did was set the Arizona total offense record of 368 yards, 338 of it passing. That's 'Bear Down!'"

GEORGE ROUNTREE III,
Rountree & Seagle, Attorneys

UA's prospects for 1992-93 brightened when Chris Mills opted to bypass the NBA draft and return to campus for his senior year. In 1991-92 Mills was All Pac-10, All-District 8 and All-America honorable mention. *Photo: Scott Borden. Courtesy, University Photo Center.*

ARIZONA
42

HADIE REDD IS FIRST BLACK BASKETBALL LETTERMAN

In 1951 Hadie Redd became UA's first black basketball player and in 1955 he became its first black letterman. He had come to Tucson out of Phoenix segregated Carver High School mainly because of Judge Hayzel Daniels, another great black athlete who years earlier had been denied a varsity uniform.

Daniels played a pivotal part in guiding Hadie Redd to the UA. A great football player at Tucson High, Daniels was allowed to play freshman UA football but not varsity. Nearly 25 years later he helped break the school's color line in athletics.

Daniels became a successful Phoenix attorney and the state's first black Magistrate Judge.

Hadie Redd moved to Phoenix from Tyler, Texas, in the mid-1940s when his father found employment as a maintenance man.

"I watched the freshman basketball team at Carver High," Redd recalled, "and all I wanted was to become a manager or trainer. But a friend talked me into trying out."

Redd made the team, and Coach Joe Flipper took the youth and gave him his basketball training.

Fred Enke took a look at Redd and made him a starter on the frosh team. He may have been the first black on the Arizona hardwoods, but he had no problems:

"I had played in high school against some of the Wildcat players and had no problems with the players," said Redd. "And Coach Enke helped me considerably. I owe an awful lot to him."

Redd had a standout career in basketball. Later he became the chief investigator for the San Francisco District Attorney's Office, the first black to ever hold the position.

Hadie Redd takes control of the basketball court. *Courtesy, University of Arizona Athletic Department.*

secutive victory streak at McKale Center, which ranks as the 10th longest in college basketball history. It began with the first game of the 1987-88 season with a 94-62 victory over Long Beach State and was finally ended on January 11, 1992, by UCLA, 89-87. The 71-game streak included only games against collegiate teams, while only 62 games of the school-record 81-game home-court streak posted by Fred Enke's teams from 1945-52 were against collegiate competition. During the 71-game streak, the Wildcats also won 41 consecutive Pac-10 games, at home, and under Olson have won more than 90 percent of league games in McKale.

Olson's nine-year record at Arizona of 214-75 (.740) and 19-year career mark of 405-169 (.706) put him among the elite in the college coaching ranks. Over the past five years his record of 141-31—an average of 28-plus wins per season and an .820 percentage—ranks the UA as one of the top three winningest programs in the country. In McKale Center he has never had a losing record, posted five undefeated seasons, and overall is 125-16, an amazing winning percentage of nearly 89 percent.

The silver-maned Swede from Minnesota has built his legacy at Arizona on the bedrock of sound recruiting, fundamental and intelligent play and rugged scheduling, dominating the Pac-10 and taking Wildcat basketball into the national limelight as one of the country's premier programs.

UNIVERSITY OF ARIZONA MEN'S BASKETBALL STATISTICAL HIGHLIGHTS

Year	Coach	W-L	Conf.# W-L	Pl.	NCAA/NIT W-L
1904-05	Orin A. Kates	1-0			
1905-06	Orin A. Kates	0-0			
1906-07	Unknown	3-1			
1907-08	Unknown	1-2			
1908-09	Unknown	1-1			
1909-10	Unknown	2-2			
1910-11	Unknown	3-0			
1911-12	Frank L. Kleeberger	2-2			
1912-13	Raymond L. Quigley	3-2			
1913-14	Raymond L. Quigley	7-2			
1914-15	J.F. McKale	9-0			
1915-16	J.F. McKale	5-0			
1916-17	J.F. McKale	10-2			
1917-18	J.F. McKale	3-2			
1918-19	J.F. McKale	6-3			
1919-20	J.F. McKale	9-5			
1920-21	J.F. McKale	7-0			
1921-22	James H. Pierce	10-2			
1922-23	James H. Pierce	17-3			
1923-24	Basil Stanley	14-3			
1924-25	Walter Davis	7-4			
1925-26	Fred A. Enke	6-7			
1926-27	Fred A. Enke	13-4			
1927-28	Fred A. Enke	13-3			
1928-29	Fred A. Enke	19-4			
1929-30	Fred A. Enke	15-6			
1930-31	Fred A. Enke	9-6			
1931-32	Fred A. Enke	18-2			
1932-33	Fred A. Enke	19-5	7-3		
1933-34	Fred A. Enke	18-9	9-3	2	
1934-35	Fred A. Enke	11-8	5-7	4	
1935-36	Fred A. Enke	16-7	11-5	1	
1936-37	Fred A. Enke	14-11	9-7	3	
1937-38	Fred A. Enke	13-8	9-7	2	
1938-39	Fred A. Enke	12-11	8-10	5	
1939-40	Fred A. Enke	15-10	12-4	1	
1940-41	Fred A. Enke	11-7	9-6	2	
1941-42	Fred A. Enke	9-13	6-10	6	
1942-43	Fred A. Enke	22-2	16-2	1T	
1943-44.	Fred A. Enke	12-2			
1944-45	Fred A. Enke	7-11			
1945-46	Fred A. Enke	25-5	14-3	1	0-1(NIT)
1946-47	Fred A. Enke	21-3	14-2		
1947-48	Fred A. Enke	19-10	12-4	1	0-2
1948-49	Fred A. Enke	17-11	13-3	1	1-1
1949-50	Fred A. Enke	26-5	14-2	1	0-1(NIT)
1950-51	Fred A. Enke	24-6	15-1	1	0-1;0-1(NIT)
1951-52	Fred A. Enke	11-16	6-8	3T	
1952-53	Fred A. Enke	14-13	11-3	1T	
1953-54	Fred A. Enke	14-10	8-4	3	
1954-55	Fred A. Enke	8-17	3-9	6	
1955-56	Fred A. Enke	11-15	6-6	5	
1956-57	Fred A. Enke	13-13	5-5	3	
1957-58	Fred A. Enke	10-15	4-6	4T	
1958-59	Fred A. Enke	4-22	1-9	6	
1959-60	Fred A. Enke	10-14	4-6	4	
1960-61	Fred A. Enke	11-15	5-5	3	
1961-62	Bruce Larson	12-14			
1962-63	Bruce Larson	13-13	3-7	5T	
1963-64	Bruce Larson	15-11	4-6	4T	
1964-65	Bruce Larson	17-9	5-5	2T	
1965-66	Bruce Larson	15-11	5-5	3T	
1966-67	Bruce Larson	8-17	3-7	5	
1967-68	Bruce Larson	11-13	4-6	4T	
1968-69	Bruce Larson	17-10	5-5	3T	
1969-70	Bruce Larson	12-14	8-6	4	
1970-71	Bruce Larson	10-16	3-11	8	
1971-72	Bruce Larson	6-20	4-10	7	
1972-73	Fred Snowden	16-10	9-5	2T	
1973-74	Fred Snowden	19-7	9-5	2T	
1974-75	Fred Snowden	22-7	9-5	3	
1975-76	Fred Snowden	24-9	11-3	1	2-1
1976-77	Fred Snowden	21-6	10-4	2	0-1
1977-78	Fred Snowden	15-11	6-8	4T	
1978-79	Fred Snowden	16-11	10-8	4T	
1979-80	Fred Snowden	12-15	6-12	6	
1980-81	Fred Snowden	13-14	8-10	5T	
1981-82	Fred Snowden	9-18	4-14	8T	
1982-83	Ben Lindsey	4-24	1-17	10	
1983-84	Lute Olson	11-17	8-10	8T	
1984-85	Lute Olson	21-10	12-6	3T	0-1
1985-86	Lute Olson	23-9	14-4	1	0-1
1986-87	Lute Olson	18-12	13-5	2	0-1
1987-88	Lute Olson	35-3	17-1	1	4-1
1988-89	Lute Olson	29-4	17-1	1	2-1
1989-90	Lute Olson	25-7	15-3	1T	1-1
1990-91	Lute Olson	28-7	14-4	1	2-1
1991-92	Lute Olson	24-7	13-5	3	0-1

+ One tie

#-intrasquad game only

** Border Conference, 1932-61; Western Athletic Conference, 1962-78; Pacific 10 Conference, 1978-present*

CAREER TOP TEN

Scoring Average		
23.9	Coniel Norman	1973-74
19.9	Joe Skaisgir	1960-62
19.2	Sean Elliott	1986-89
18.7	Bob Elliott	1974-77
18.6	Bill Warner	1968-71
18.6	Eric Money	1973-74
17.8	Ernie McCray	1957-60
16.8	Joe Nehls	1977-80
16.4	Bill Davis	1966-68
16.3	Ron Davis	1979-81

SEASON TOP TEN

Scoring Average		
24.0	Coniel Norman	1972-73
23.9	Ernie McCray	1959-60
23.8	Coniel Norman	1973-74
23.3	Bob Elliott	1974-75
22.2	Sean Elliott	1988-89
20.9	Bill Warner	1970-71
20.3	Joe Skaisgir	1961-62
20.3	Bill Warner	1969-70
20.0	Herman Harris	1976-77
19.8	Al Fleming	1974-75

From interclass sandlot games to national championships—that is the saga of baseball at the University of Arizona. No other sport has achieved the consistent success and recognition that baseball has for the university. The first team was formed in 1898, playing four games against a Tucson town team. In those early days of the sport it was not unusual for preps and faculty members to play, and the designations of "coach" and "captain" were often interchangeable. The first intercollegiate and the first out-of-town competition took place in 1907, the

PLAY BALL!

UA baseball teams have won three national championships and have been to the College World Series 14 times. *Photo: Chris Mooney/Balfour Walker. Concept: Dave Sitton. Courtesy, University of Arizona Athletic Department.*

UA losing three of four games in a home-and-home series with Tempe Normal.

In 1908 the UA team claimed the state championship, sweeping three games from Tempe and setting off a wave of enthusiasm on campus and in Tucson for baseball. However, until 1920, the only collegiate opponent was Tempe Normal. The two state rivals played 24 games.

The 1909 Arizona baseball team, with captain Burrell Hatcher, middle row, second from right, posed in the studio. *Courtesy, Special Collections, University of Arizona Library.*

In 1916, one of the UA's great all-around athletes of the times, Asa Porter, pitched a no-hitter against Tempe, winning 5-1 and striking out 14. From 1907 through 1919, the UA held a narrow 13-11 edge over their archrivals.

The first out-of-state competition came in 1914 from a barnstorming University of Hawaii "Chinese" nine that dropped the Cats in two games.

J. F. "Pop" McKale became the team's first full-time coach in 1915, and would serve in that capacity, with the exception of 1920-21, for 33 seasons until 1950.

Probably the biggest game for UA baseball in the early years came in April 1919 when a game was played with the Chicago Cubs, who the year before had won the World Series. The Wildcats lost, 7-3, but turned in such a good showing that they got some good write-ups in the Chicago papers. Pitching for the Wildcats that day was A. L. "Slony" Slonaker, Arizona's best pitcher during his five years in school.

Asa Porter took over the head coaching duties during the 1920-21 season and beat USC two out of three times.

In 1920, the Wildcats won nine and lost one against an all-collegiate schedule that included Tempe, USC and Stanford. Top pitcher for that year and for the next few years was Andy Tolson, father of Brad Tolson, who compiled a great record for the Wildcats in 1951. In 1924, the USC Trojans were swept by the Cats and Cliff "Chick" Morfield delivered a no-hit game against Arizona State, winning 5-0 at Tempe. In 1925 Andy Tolson captained the 1925 squad that again defeated USC, this time in three straight games. It was not until 1926 that Southern California would take the season series with the Wildcats, winning two out of three at Tucson—their first winning series in six years. By this time baseball games were being played on the new field at the east end of campus. Arizona's best player in 1926 was fiery catcher John "Button" Salmon, whose clutch two-base hit drove in the winning run in UA's lone win over the Trojans. A few days later Salmon was elected student body president, and that game-winning hit became known as "the 200-vote double." Arizona's starting quarterback in football, Salmon was fatally injured in an automobile accident following the first game of the 1926 season.

With the university's nearly finished gymnasium in the background, the 1926 baseball team posed for a team picture. Standing at the right is coach J.F. McKale, and kneeling in front of him is three-year starting catcher John "Button" Salmon, who a few months later would become the center of one of the greatest traditions in intercollegiate sport. *Photo: Albert Buchman. Courtesy, Special Collections, University of Arizona Library.*

In 1927 the Wildcats played their first series with UCLA, taking all three games. With the exception of 1926, the California teams never came close to taking a series from the Cats. As McKale put it: "No college team except Texas has ever held an edge on us." The Chicago Cubs did maintain their dominance over the Arizona squad, however. In 1929, they walloped the Cats, 14-4. Arizona's only other pre-war major league competition was a 14-4 defeat at the hands of the Pittsburgh Pirates in 1939.

Financial difficulties hampered baseball scheduling during the early depression years, and only two games were played in 1931. Out-of-state collegiate competition was curtailed until 1934. USC was played only once (1936) until after World War II.

Two of McKale's great players of the '30s were Hank Lieber, who became the school's first major leaguer in 1933 when he signed with the New York Giants, and Hal Warnock, 1935, who went with the St. Louis Browns. Lieber would play ten years in the majors with the Giants and Cubs and play in three All-Star games.

Recalling his playing days in Arizona, Warnock remembered Wildcat catcher Frank Sancet, who later served as UA head coach from 1950 until 1972. "A runner on third had better be well ahead of the baseball when Frank Sancet was blocking the plate or he could suffer serious injuries," Warnock once said. "Sancet was tough, fierce and softspoken, with a terrible temper."

This early baseball game (circa 1926-27) has home plate facing southwest. Behind the first baseman, a fence juts out about 20 feet before heading straight out to right field. Imagine the ground rules dealing with this condition! *Courtesy, University of Arizona Athletic Department.*

From 1934-38 McKale's record was 88-13-2 and Arizona generally was considered the premier collegiate team in the Southwest. The 1942 squad chalked up an 18-1 record, but the following year they were 12-10.

Baseball was cancelled during 1944-45 due to the war. Following the war, the explosion of enrollment and growth of the university athletic program demanded more and more of McKale's time as athletic director. After the 1949 season the gray-haired, bespectacled coach of Arizona baseball for some 33 seasons finally decided to step down from coaching to devote himself full-time to his administrative duties.

Frank Sancet: 1950-1972

McKale's personal pick to succeed him was UA grad Frank Sancet, who had not only caught for "Pop" in 1929, but was also a standout in football and basketball before leaving school to play minor league baseball.

If McKale laid the foundation for UA baseball, it was Sancet who became the master builder of the program.

In his first season he came within a game of taking the Wildcats to the College World Series in Omaha, losing a three-game NCAA District 6 playoff at Austin to defending NCAA champion Texas, which would go on to its second national title. The lightly regarded Wildcats shocked the Longhorns 5-4 in the first game, lost a close 9-8 decision in the second and were beaten 7-3 in the deciding game. Sancet's first squad also produced Arizona's first All-Americans, catcher Bob Murray (first team) and first baseman Tony Morales.

Sancet would continue to battle the Southwest Conference champion for the District 6 College World Series (CWS) berth, losing to Texas A&M in 1951, and to Texas in 1952 and 1953. In 1954 Arizona was reassigned to District 7 and earned its first trip to Omaha by sweeping Colorado State College and Wyoming in playoffs held in Greeley, Colorado, and Laramie, Wyoming.

Arizona's CWS debut was an impressive one. The Wildcats defeated Oregon 12-1 as Carl Thomas pitched a complete game and hit two home runs to drive in seven runs. However, despite excellent pitching by Thomas and Donnie Lee, the Wildcats were eliminated by heartbreaking losses to Michigan State, 2-1, and Oklahoma State, 5-4 in 14 innings.

QUOTABLES

"A. G. Edwards & Sons is proud to support UA athletics. Bruce Ferguson, a broker here for more than 10 years, was a pitcher on the 1976 championship baseball team. As a result, many of our employees follow UA baseball and cheer for the Wildcats."

DANIEL D'ANTIMO,
Vice President,
A. G. Edwards & Sons, Inc.

In 1955 the UA was back in District 6, but beat out Texas A&M to earn a second straight trip to Omaha. At the CWS, the Cats bounced back from an opening-game 4-1 loss to Western Michigan to defeat Springfield, 6-0 on a two-hit, 15-strikeout effort by Thomas, and then roughed up Colorado State, 20-0. For the second straight year, an extra-inning 5-4 loss to Oklahoma State, this time in 12 innings, would send the UA home. Thomas earned first-team All-America honors, and first baseman Russ Gragg (second) and third baseman Craig Sorenson (third) also garnered All-America recognition.

The 1956 team ranks with the 1959 and 1963 squads as Sancet's finest. All three made it to the championship game of the College World Series only to have to settle for the runner-up trophy.

Frank Sancet: The Gray Fox of Arizona Baseball

In 1949, 35 years after he had come to the UA, McKale closed out his active coaching career and began to look for the man he wanted as his replacement. He had the world to choose from, but his first and only choice was Frank (Pancho) Sancet, a tough kid who had played Wildcat football and baseball for McKale.

At the time McKale said of Sancet: "There never was a harder working player or a harder working coach. He's going to make a great college coach."

The prediction proved true. Sancet had a remarkable career, winning 831 games (831-282-8), and built the Arizona program into a national power, taking nine teams to the College World Series and 17 of his 22 teams into the post-season.

"Pop McKale once told me I would never make a good ball player because I wouldn't chew tobacco," Sancet once recalled. "Guess that's why I'm coaching instead of playing professional baseball."

Before turning to coaching, the native Arizonan had three years of duty in pro baseball. After graduation from the UA in 1932, he signed as a catcher with Tampa, Florida, of the Class B Southeastern League. The following year he returned to Tucson.

As a coach he demanded toughness and dedication. If there was one flaw in Frank Sancet's makeup it was that he constantly down-played the outstanding job he did in his 22 seasons at the UA.

Frank Sancet
Courtesy, University of Arizona Athletic Department.

In 1956, led by All-American pitchers Thomas and Don Lee, the Wildcats met Minnesota three times at Omaha, falling to the Golden Gophers in the title game, 12-1. Ironically, one of the stars of that Minnesota squad was an All-American shortstop and future major leaguer named Jerry Kindall.

In 1959, behind the All-American play of left fielder Matt Encinas, catcher Allen Hall and second baseman Chuck Shoemaker, Sancet's squad went all the way to the final game, losing 5-3 to its old CWS nemesis, Oklahoma State.

In the mid-50s, Carl Thomas, 6'5", 245 pounds, intimidated baseball foes with his pitching prowess and his size. In 1956 he threw back-to-back no hitters against ASU (7-0) and UCLA (10-0). In the UCLA game, he broke a Bruin's arm with his first pitch. *Courtesy, University of Arizona Athletic Department.*

In the 1963 College World Series, the UA romped to four straight victories before having its NCAA title hopes again derailed, this time by USC, 6-4 and 5-3.

Sancet would continue to field strong teams during the next decade, going to the CWS in 1966 and 1970. He produced some of the UA's great diamond stars, including two-time first-team All-America infielder Eddie Leon, who would go on to an eight-year major league career with the Indians, White Sox and Yankees; major league pitchers Mike Paul and Tim Plodinec; and two of the school's best-ever hitters, Jerry Stitt and Steve Mikulic, both first-team All-Americans.

When Sancet retired at age 65 following the 1972 season, it was the end of a coaching career that few would ever hope to equal. In 23 seasons he had taken his Wildcat teams into post-season play 16 times, including nine College World Series. At the time of his retirement, he was the all-time leader among college coaches in total wins with a record of 835-282-8. Twenty-six of his players had earned All-America honors, including 15 first-team selections, and 14 played in the major leagues.

One of the great legacies of the Sancet era is the baseball facility named in his honor. With the exception of several playoff and other important matches held at Hi Corbet Field, games from

THE SANCET SHIFT

The Sancet Shift—the clever strategy Sancet sometimes used in bunt situations—worked to perfection against Arizona State in 1961.

In the 1961 match, Arizona was leading 3-1 when the Sun Devils put the first two batters on in the seventh inning. Up came pitcher Roger Barnson. It was a dangerous bunt situation. If Barnson bunted successfully, Arizona State would have had the tying run in scoring position.

It was at that point Sancet pulled his quizzical shift. The third baseman and first baseman moved close to the batter to handle the probable bunt. The second baseman covered first and the shortstop covered third. Center field was left open as Bill Barraclough came in to cover second.

Barnson, seeing the shift that dared him to bunt, swung away and hit a pop fly to right field. He couldn't bunt and he couldn't resist a shot at the open field in center. But he proved he was a pitcher, not a hitter.

The Sun Devils were shut out the rest of the way and Arizona won the critical game, 3-1.

"It was percentage ball to bunt, and we had to change their strategy," Sancet explained at the time. "That's why we went into the shift. It worked and that's what counted."

In 1950 Arizona pulled the same type of shift against Texas and was so successful that Texas then used it against Minnesota. Minnesota then used it against someone else in a tournament.

SHORTEST COACHING CAREER IN UA HORSEHIDE HISTORY

The record books don't show it, but the great Hank Lieber was the coach of the Arizona baseball team for three weeks in 1936.

One of the most successful ball players ever turned out by the UA, Lieber signed with the New York Giants and in 1935 hit .331 with 22 home runs and 107 RBIs.

Disgusted with the Giants' new contract that winter, he declared himself a hold-out and Coach McKale stepped in.

"Let's announce that you're the new baseball coach at the University of Arizona," McKale suggested. "They'll give you a raise once they think you're not coming back."

Lieber jumped at the idea and for a couple of weeks he ran the Wildcat ball club practice. He stayed in shape by belting baseballs out of the park as the players stood by in awe.

On March 16, the Giants management contacted him and two days later he signed and McKale resumed as baseball coach.

McKale loved to say: "I guess Hank gained about $3,000 by playing 'coach' for three weeks."

Lieber originally signed with the Giants in 1931 and spent the next two years playing for their farm teams. In 1933 he was called up to play in the World Series with the Giants and appeared in six games.

Lieber then had five slugging years with the Giants. His best was .331 in 1935. He was traded to the Cubs in 1939, playing three seasons there before returning to the Giants for his last big league year in 1942.

Lieber's lifetime stats included a .288 batting average with 101 homers and 519 RBIs.

1930 through 1966 were played on the forty-year-old, unlit varsity diamond just east of Bear Down Gym. In 1967 Wildcat Field, located east of Arizona Stadium and south of what would eventually be the site of McKale Center, opened. However, night games were still played at Hi Corbet until 1975, when a major modernization program was completed. It included lights and a 9,000 capacity stadium with an enclosed press box, making the field one of college baseball's showcase ballparks. On April 19, 1986, Wildcat Field was officially dedicated and renamed Frank Sancet Field in honor of the former coach, who died on March 22, 1985, at the age of 77.

JERRY KINDALL: 1973-PRESENT

Chosen to carry on the Sancet legacy was a name familiar to Arizona baseball fans. It was the same Jerry Kindall who had led Minnesota to the 1956 NCAA title over Arizona. After eight years in the majors, Kindall had served as an assistant coach at his alma mater since 1966 before being hired to replace Sancet.

Kindall went right to work at challenging archrival Arizona State, which under Coach Bobby Winkles had

J.F. McKale achieved his greatest coaching distinction as UA's baseball coach. Henry "Hank" Lieber, a pitcher/outfielder, was probably his greatest player. He made the majors in 1933 and played 10 seasons as a home-run-hitting outfielder. *Courtesy, Special Collections, University of Arizona Library.*

UA Head Baseball Coach

Jerry Kindall
Courtesy, University of Arizona Athletic Department.

When a player arrives at the UA to play for Jerry Kindall, he is taught more than baseball. He also learns responsibility.

Jerry Kindall, widely respected in the coaching profession, is not only a coach to his players but a teacher as well. And his loyalty to his coaching assistants, players and the UA is solid and unquestionable.

When the UA hired the 36-year-old former major-leaguer as head baseball coach, there were 100 applicants for the job. Kindall was the unanimous choice of the selection committee.

"I always wanted to be a college coach," Kindall says, "but I never expected to land at such an outstanding university."

When Kindall was hired in 1973, then athletic director Dick Clausen prophesied: "From all reports, we have in Jerry Kindall a man who will give Arizona championship baseball."

Sure enough, three seasons later Kindall's Cats won the NCAA title and added a second championship in 1980, making him the only man to ever play on a College World Series championship team (Minnesota in 1956) and also coach one. Ironically, the '56 Gopher team beat Arizona to win the title.

Kindall's team again took it all in 1986. Only one other college coach has won more NCAA titles than Kindall, who shares his niche with Dick Siebert of Minnesota (3) and Bobby Winkles of ASU.

Arizona sand first filled Kindall's shoes as a major-league shortstop. After his 1956 All America season, he attended spring training in Mesa with the Chicago Cubs and in Tucson with the Cleveland Indians.

Kindall was with the Cleveland Indians in 1962, when they were still a respectable ball club and could give the New York Yankees a stiff battle. The classy infielder, who had the most graceful fielding moves in the business at that time, was not a great hitter, except against the Yankees.

In May 1962 the Indians played a series in Yankee Stadium, and Mickey Mantle, the great Yankee outfielder, spent the Easter weekend chasing hits off the bat of Jerry Kindall. In the Yankee clubhouse after the series, Mantle sat in front of his locker pulling off his stockings and rubbing his tired; sore legs.

"Why didn't those guys leave Kindall in the National League?" he grumbled.

The following month the Yankees came to Cleveland on Friday the 13th of June. They were leading the Indians by two games. Kindall had three hits in the first game of the series, two more in the second game, and in a Sunday double header he hit a home run in each game as the Indians swept the series and took over first place.

After his final big-league season, in 1965 with the American League champion Minnesota Twins, Kindall coached at his alma mater, the University of Minnesota for six years.

During the off-season he earned his undergraduate degree in English and a master's in physical education.

Kindall is nationally known for his teaching skills and wrote two books on the fundamentals of baseball which were published in 1983. He recently produced an instructional video and has served as an analyst for ESPN.

By the end of the 1990 season, Kindall had taken 10 teams to postseason play, while five have reached Omaha. Along the way he has coached 18 All America players and guided more than 100 young men into the professional ranks. He's earned National Coach of the Year honors three times (1976, 1980, 1986).

Kindall was inducted into the American Baseball Coaches Association of America Hall of Fame in January 1990. With more than 700 college victories—all at the UA—he is widely recognized as one of the winningest college coaches. Kindall was Pacific-10 Coach of the Year in 1980 and 1989, and *Sporting News* Coach of the Year in 1976 and 1980.

One of the country's leading proponents of baseball on all levels, and one of the country's gentlemen of the game, Kindall is active in the Fellowship of Christian Athletes and the Young Life campaign.

Jerry Kindall stands tall and it isn't only because he's 6-2. In nearly two decades as a UA coach, Kindall has never been linked to controversy. That's pretty unusual in collegiate athletics today.

superseded Arizona as the dominant college baseball power in the WAC and Southwest/Rocky Mountain region and had won three NCAA titles.

Kindall's second team may have been the best college team ever to not win a national title. Led by three-time All-Americans Ron Hassey and Dave Stegman—then just sophomores, but arguably among the best players ever to wear UA baseball uniforms—the 1974 Wildcats rewrote the school record books while rolling to their first WAC title and first three-game sweep of ASU since 1970.

Arizona took a gaudy 56-4 record, still the most wins by any Arizona team, into post-season play, where the Cats rolled over BYU in the WAC playoff at Provo. But then, in a stunning upset, Northern Colorado defeated Arizona, 6-5 and 6-2, to win the NCAA Division 7 title and cancel the Wildcats' tickets for Omaha. It was the first time in league history that a WAC team had not advanced to the College World Series.

However, within two years the Wildcats would be golden. In 1976, Arizona lost six regular season games to Arizona State, but a 52-16 regular season record would earn them an NCAA at-large playoff berth. After sweeping the NCAA Midwest Regional, the UA opened in Omaha against, who else, ASU, and lost again. Battling back through the loser's bracket, the Wildcats would win four straight, finally breaking their ASU jinx with a 5-1 victory, and then taking the measure of Eastern Michigan, 7-1, for Arizona's first NCAA team title in any sport.

QUOTABLES

"On June 9, 1986, my wife, Bethe, and I were about to welcome our firstborn into the world. The Bat Cats were playing for the national championship in Omaha. My wife permitted me to check out the score between contractions. At 4:36 p.m., Katrina was born and the Cats became national champions."

CHRIS S. LACEY,
CHA General Manager,
Radisson Suite Hotel

Pitcher/DH Steve Powers was the MVP of the series and the winning pitcher with a four-hitter against ASU. He was joined on the all-tournament team by Bob Chaulk, who was 3-0 in the series with a six-hitter against EMU; Peter Van Horne, who collected a series-record 13 hits; and Stegman and Hassey.

In 1978 the Wildcats just missed a trip to Omaha, losing to USC 2-1 in the West Regional final. But the following season, Arizona marked its first season in the Pac-10 Southern Division (Six-Pac) by earning another CWS berth. This time, after an opening win over Miami (Fla.) 5-1, the Cats were unceremoniously sent home with two straight losses, including a 16-3 pasting by eventual

GREAT MOMENTS

The University of Arizona Wildcat baseball team has come back through the loser's bracket three times at the College World Series to win the championship. Those teams had a dedication to excellence all the way to the last pitch, the last out. Southwest Hazard Control is dedicated to providing solutions to environment concerns in an efficient, effective and ethical manner. Their operating resources consist of three major divisions: asbestos abatement, hazardous waste management, and technical services. Southwest Hazard Control has the technological skill and experience to analyze an environmental problem and outline corrective options that are economical as well as effective.

Gerald Karches
President,
Southwest Hazard Control, Inc.

Cats Take College World Series Title Three Times

Considering how many universities play baseball and the quality of the competition, just reaching the College World Series is a credit to any team.

The University of Arizona Wildcats have been to the College World Series on 14 occasions. Three times the Wildcats came back through the losers bracket to win the championship game.

Only one other coach, Rod Dedeaux of USC, has won more NCAA titles than Jerry Kindall, who shares his phenomenal record of three national championships with Dick Siebert of Minnesota and Bobby Winkles, former Arizona State coach.

Title #1: The Wildcats finished the 1976 season with a 56-17 record, the second highest victory total in Arizona history. That year's team was the first in any sport at Arizona to win a national championship. All-Americans Ron Hassey and Dave Stegman led the Cats to a 7-1 victory over Eastern Michigan in the championship game.

Both Hassey and Stegman went on to major league fame. Hassey has started as catcher for the Cleveland Indians, Chicago Cubs, New York Yankees, Chicago White Sox, Oakland A's and Montreal Expos. Stegman had stints as an outfielder with the Detroit Tigers and the Chicago White Sox.

Title #2: The 1980 baseball team was nicknamed the "Cardiac Cats," because, like UA's 1961 football team, it often battled from behind to win. This group of gutsy Wildcats completed the season with a 45-21-1 record. Terry Francona, the Golden Spikes Award winner for 1980, led the Cats with a .458 average in Omaha and was selected the College World Series Most Valuable Player.

Francona's major league career included service as an out-

champion Cal State-Fullerton.

After tying California for the Six-Pac title in 1980, Arizona again returned to Omaha after sweeping the West Regional in Tucson. Once more, Kindall's squad had to battle through the loser's bracket after dropping a 6-1 opener to St. John's. But, behind the sensational play of tournament MVP and collegiate Player of the Year Terry Francona, the Cats rallied to win four straight, beating Hawaii on Scott

Speedy infielder Chuck Shoemaker earned All America honors three years in a row (1959-61) and at two different positions, second base and shortstop. He led the Wildcats to post-season play all three seasons and twice to the College World Series. Shoemaker's coach, Frank Sancet, called him the best collegiate infielder he'd ever seen. *Courtesy, University of Arizona Athletic Department.*

fielder-infielder with the Montreal Expos, Chicago Cubs and Cincinnati Reds.

Several other members of the 1980 squad also made major league rosters. Pitcher Greg Barger started for the Montreal Expos and John Moses played centerfield for the Seattle Mariners. Pitcher Craig Lefferts has had an outstanding career with the Chicago Cubs, San Francisco Giants and, currently, the San Diego Padres.

During the 1989 major league World Series it was Cat vs. Cat. Ron Hassey was behind the plate for the Oakland A's and Craig Lefferts was a Giants relief pitcher.

Title #3: The 1986 team exhibited a fearsome blend of power and speed while they chalked up a 49-19 record for the season. The Cats hit 74 home runs, paced by Todd Trafton's 15 roundtrippers, while Tommy Hinzo added a school record 45 stolen bases as the Cats tallied 147 thefts for the season.

UA left fielder Mike Senne was named the College World Series' most valuable player following the final game of the series. He had two home runs in the series, including the game-winning blast in UA's championship victory over Florida State.

Hinzo was drafted as a infielder with the Cleveland Indians in 1987. Among the other members of the 1986 team drafted were third baseman Chip Hale (Minnesota Twins) and shortstop Dave Rhode (Houston Astros).

The 1986 baseball team's national championship was a fitting end to a tremendous year for Wildcat revenue sports. In 1985-86 Arizona and Louisiana State University were the only two schools to accomplish the rare triple—send teams to the Baseball College World Series, NCAA Men's Basketball Tournament and a football bowl game. Coach Jerry Kindall reflected on the talent that helped him realize three national championships.

"We had some outstanding players who made it to the big leagues and were All-Americans here," Kindall says. "But, you know, the heart of the program is the host of average players who tried so hard, overachieved and gave it their best ... they are the heart of the team.

"You need the stars—like Hinzo, Hale, Stegman, Hassey, Francona, Lefferts—to win championships, but they need guys who are the pluggers, the doers, survivors. That's the core of any program."

Fittingly, all three championship baseball teams are in the University of Arizona Sports Hall of Fame.

Outfielder Dave Shermet's dramatic two-strike, two-out, two-run, pinch-hit home run in the bottom of the ninth gave Arizona an 8-7 victory over Maine. ***Courtesy, University of Arizona Athletic Department.***

Stanley's grand-slam homer, 6-4, in 11 innings, and reaching the championship game with a stirring 11-10 victory over Cal, scoring two runs in the bottom of the ninth.

Arizona defeated Hawaii, 5-3, in the championship game. Future major leaguers Craig Lefferts and Greg Barger, who allowed two earned runs in 26 innings between them, were joined on the all-tourney team by first-baseman Wes Clements.

It would be five years before the Wildcats would be back in Omaha again, but in 1985 they took their quickest exit ever, losing to Texas 2-1, despite a four-hitter by Joe Magrane, and then 9-3 to Stanford. That proved to be just a warm-up for the following year, when Kindall's charges would win it all for the third time.

The Cats got a scare in the 1986 CWS opener, when they came

N O T A B L E S

This cartoon by Bob White in 1951 sought to demonstrate that if loyal Wildcats were asleep on the job, innocent high schoolers might be lured by the devil—the Sun Devil—to attend Arizona State!

Courtesy, University of Arizona Athletic Department.

16

Catcher Ron Hassey, with 13 years of major league play, had the longest run in "The Bigs" of any UA alumnus. Here he applies the tag to a Clemson runner in the 1976 College World Series, where UA won its first national championship. *Courtesy, Arizona Alumni Association.*

back, after trailing Maine 7-0 late in the game, to win 8-7 on Dave Shermet's two-out, two-run pinch-hit homer in the bottom of the ninth, perhaps the most dramatic event in UA athletic history. Arizona also had to rally for wins over Loyola Marymount, 7-5, and pre-tournament favorite Florida State, 9-5, but was assured of a spot in the title game despite a 4-2 loss to defending champion Miami (Florida). In the championship game against FSU, Gary Alexander pitched a shutout for eight innings, and home runs by Series MVP Mike Senne and Gar Millay paced a 10-2 Wildcat victory.

After his worst Six-Pac record ever in 1988 (10-20), Kindall pulled off the "worst to first" trick in 1989, posting his best Six-Pac record ever at 23-7 and earning a number one ranking in the polls. It looked like the Wildcats would be back on their way to Omaha again behind future major league 20-game winner Scott Erickson, who posted a school-record 18 victories. But at the West I Regional in Tucson, Long Beach State ambushed the home team, beating the Wildcats twice to earn the CWS trip. Erickson and power-hitting catcher Alan Zinter, who tied the school record with 18 homers and led the Six-Pac with 81 RBIs, both earned first-team All-America honors.

Uncharacteristic losing records followed in 1990 and 1991. But a Kindall-led team is never down for long, and in 1992 the Wildcats went from worst to first again, winning the Six-Pac with an 18-12 record in the closest race in league history. It took a season-ending sweep of Arizona State, their first since 1986, to do it. The UA again hosted the West Regional, but was too good a host, exiting early with surprising upset losses to Washington, 6-5, and Hawaii, 10-3. Regional winner Pepperdine would go on to win the College World Series.

After more than 90 years, baseball is now well established at the University of Arizona as

Slick-fielding junior shortstop Chris Gump helped stabilize the Wildcat infield in 1992 and was the Six-Pac runner-up in hitting at .376. *Photo: Robert F. Walker.*

When he was named All America, In 1965 John Fouse's 12-2 record led the nation's college pitchers. Remarkably, six of those wins were shutouts, which ranks second on the UA career list. When not on the mound, Fouse was in the outfield. A devastating power hitter, he turned many games around with home runs. *Courtesy, University of Arizona Athletic Department.*

UA Gets First World Record

Hugh McMullan was a sophomore playing shortstop in 1952 when he gave the University of Arizona its first world record.

McMullan, who weighed 165 pounds and stood 5' 10", whipped the baseball 427¼ feet in a measured test during an annual baseball field games competition. The throw wiped out world records in amateur, collegiate and professional classes. The previous record was 426 feet 9¼ inches, set in 1910.

Because of his extraordinary heave-ho, McMullan won a test as a pitcher on the Wildcat ball club. However, his lack of accuracy prompted Coach Frank Sancet to leave him on the roster as an infielder.

Prior to setting the new world record, McMullan, while standing flat-footed at home plate, threw a baseball over the center field wall in Arizona's baseball park. That's an amazing distance of 410 feet and farther than many hitters can slug the horsehide.

WORLD RECORD HOLDER—Hugh McMullan, University of ...zona, yesterday received approval for a world's record in base... throwing. He recently threw the baseball 427 feet ¼ inch. ...e previous world's record of 426 feet 9½ inches was set back in ...910. McMullan will put on a demonstration of his throwing ability in Corbett field next Monday night as a preliminary to the Tucson-Juarez Sportsmen's Fund benefit game.

Arizonan's World Throwing Record Is Given Approva...

...ugh McMullan Surpasses 42-Year-Old Mark With 427 Feet Baseball Heave; to Throw At Sportsmen's Fund Exhibition

its premier intercollegiate sports program, headed up by one of the country's most respected coaches, Jerry Kindall. In 20 years in the UA dugout and in his accustomed third-base coaching box, Kindall has posted 767 victories, ranking him among the top 25 active coaches. He has taken 11 teams to postseason play, five teams to the College World Series, and has earned National Coach of the Year honors three times. In 1991 he was inducted into the American Baseball Coaches Association Hall of Fame. He has coached 18 All-America players and sent 111 young men into the professional ranks, 24 of whom have played in the major leagues.

Sophomore Tim Schweitzer, shown here, and Mike Schiefelbein were the mainstays of the Wildcat pitching staff in 1992, pitching coach Jim Wing's 20th and last season as Jerry Kindall's right-hand man. "Winger" announced his retirement at the beginning of the season. *Photo: Robert F. Walker.*

28

University of Arizona Baseball Statistical Highlights

Seasons' Records

Year	Coach	W-L-T	Conference W-L	Conference Pl.	NCAA W-L	NCAA Pl.
1904	B.L. Cosgrove	6-1-0				
1905	R. Newton	2-2-0				
1906	B.R. Hatcher	2-0-0				
1907	R. Newton	5-4-0				
1908	B.R. Hatcher	10-2-0				
1909	Dan Farrish	unknown				
1910	R. Rigg	unknown				
1911	William Honley	2-4-0				
1912	Joe Collins	7-4-0				
1913	R.L. Quigley	1-0-0				
1914	C.R. Stewart	4-4-0				
1915	J.F. McKale	5-3-0				
1916	J.F. McKale	6-2-0				
1917	J.F. McKale	4-2-0				
1918	J.F. McKale	0-1-0				
1919	J.F. McKale	3-3-0				
1920	W.A. Porter	11-4-0				
1921	W.A. Porter	7-1-0				
1922	J.F. McKale	6-1-2				
1923	J.F. McKale	9-1-0				
1924	J.F. McKale	7-1-0				
1925	J.F. McKale	9-2-0				
1926	J.F. McKale	9-4-0				
1927	J.F. McKale	10-6-0				
1928	J.F. McKale	5-3-1				
1929	J.F. McKale	5-5-0				
1930	J.F. McKale	6-8-0				
1931	No games					
1932	J.F. McKale	4-4-0				
1933	J.F. McKale	8-6-0				
1934	J.F. McKale	17-4-3				
1935	J.F. McKale	19-1-0				
1935	J.F. McKale	19-4-0				
1937	J.F. McKale	18-2-0				
1938	J.F. McKale	15-2-2				
1939	J.F. McKale	11-7-0				
1940	J.F. McKale	11-5-1				
1941	J.F. McKale	10-9-1				
1942	J.F. McKale	18-1-0				
1943	J.F. McKale	12-10-0				
1944	No games, World War II					
1945	No games, World War II					
1946	J.F. McKale	10-3-0				
1947	J.F. McKale	15-4-0				

Year	Coach	W-L-T	Conference W-L	Conference Pl.	NCAA W-L	NCAA Pl.
1948	J.F. McKale	19-8-0				
1949	J.F. McKale	12-6-0				
1950	Frank Sancet	28-6-1			1-2	
1951	Frank Sancet	28-4-0			1-2	
1952	Frank Sancet	22-14-0			1-2	
1953	Frank Sancet	21-16-0			1-2	
1954	Frank Sancet	40-9-0				
1955	Frank Sancet	43-8-0				
1956	Frank Sancet	49-8-0				
1957	Frank Sancet	34-12-0				
1958	Frank Sancet	38-14-0				
1959	Frank Sancet	39-10-2				
1960	Frank Sancet	43-9-0				
1961	Frank Sancet	41-9-0				
1962	Frank Sancet	40-8-0				
1963	Frank Sancet	39-17-0				
1964	Frank Sancet	31-13-1				
1965	Frank Sancet	37-13-0				
1966	Frank Sancet	40-15-0				
1967	Frank Sancet	35-15-0				
1968	Frank Sancet	34-17-0				
1969	Frank Sancet	37-10-0				
1970	Frank Sancet	44-18-0				
1971	Frank Sancet	30-18-2				
1972	Frank Sancet	38-20-0				
1973	Jerry Kindall	37-16-0	15-5	2		
1974	Jerry Kindall	58-6-0	16-2	1	0-2	
1975	Jerry Kindall	43-13-1	14-4	2	0-2	
1976	Jerry Kindall	56-17-0	12-6	2	8-1	1
1977	Jerry Kindall	38-25-1	7	2		
1978	Jerry Kindall	43-13-0	13-5	2	2-2	
1979	Jerry Kindall	43-25-0	17-13	2	4-2	5
1980	Jerry Kindall	45-21-1	17-13	1	8-1	1
1981	Jerry Kindall	30-22-0	14-16	4		
1982	Jerry Kindall	32-22-0	15-14	3		
1983	Jerry Kindall	25-31-0	14-15	4		
1984	Jerry Kindall	22-36-0	11-19	5		
1985	Jerry Kindall	47-22-0	17-13	2	3-2	7
1986	Jerry Kindall	49-19-0	18-12	2	8-1	1
1987	Jerry Kindall	34-26-0	13-17	4		
1988	Jerry Kindall	33-26-0	10-20	6		
1989	Jerry Kindall	45-18-1	23-7			
1990	Jerry Kindall	26-34-0				
1991	Jerry Kindall	27-32-0	10-20	6		
1992	Jerry Kindall	34-21-1	18-2	1	0-2	
	Total	**1,956-862-20**				

University of Arizona Baseball Statistical Highlights

Individual Hitting Records

Batting Average, Career (300+ AB)

.412	Marty Hurd	1957-58	(131-318)
.406	John Glenn	1970-72	(204-503)
.399	Lloyd Jenney	1950-52	(128-321)
.394	Brad Mills	1978-79	(156-396)
.393	Steve Mikulic	1970-71	(162-412)

Home Runs, Career

34	Dave Shermet	1985-88
33	Les Pearsey	1975-78
30	Bob Woodside	1975-78
29	Alan Zinter	1987-89
28	Wes Clements	1979-80
28	Craig Sorenson	1955-57
28	Dennis Haines	1971-74

Batting Average, Season (115+ AB)

.484	Lloyd Jenney	1952	(60-124)
.473	Mary Hurd	1957	(79-167)
.438	John Glenn	1972	(96-219)
.435	Brad Mills	1978	(77-177)
.434	Tom Clarkson	1957	(79-182)

Home Runs, Season

18	Alan Zinter	1989
18	Gary Alexander	1987
17	Bob Woodside	1977
16	Les Pearsey	1978
15	Todd Trafton	1986

Individual Pitching Records (Career)

No-Hit Games

1984	Joe Magrane	4-1 vs. Cal State Fullerton
1971	Les Lisowski	5-0 vs. N. Colorado
1956	Carl Thomas	7-0 vs. ASU
1956	Carl Thomas	10-0 vs. UCLA
1916	Asa Porter	5-1 vs. ASU

Wins

36-7	Don Lee	1954-56
35-5	Carl Thomas	1954-56
33-17	Ron Sismondo	1979-82
32-8	Rich Hinton	1967-69
30-7	Jim Ward	1958-60
29-10	Dave Breuker	1972-74
29-19	Ed Vosberg	1980-83
28-12	Dave Crutcher	1976-79
28-19	Joe Magrane	1983-85
27-7	Steve Powers	1974-76
26-11	Gilbert Heredia	1986-87

Shutouts

8	Don Lee	1954-56
6	Rich Hinton	1967-69
6	John Fouse	1963-65
6	Sherwin Scott	1962-64

11
RIZONA

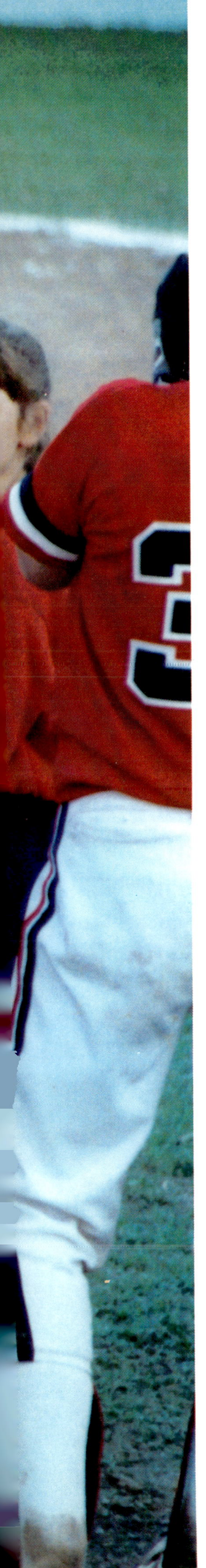

Softball is the most recent women's team sport to achieve national prominence for the University of Arizona. The school's first women's national team championship, won at the 1991 NCAA Softball College World Series in Oklahoma City, had its roots in the highly successful UA softball teams of the 1970s.

Intercollegiate competition for softball began in 1972, and two years later, under head coach Judy Spray, Arizona beat out two-time defending national champion Arizona State to qualify for its first appearance in the Softball College World Series in Omaha, Nebraska (then

LADYCATS

We're number one! That's the signal given by Wildcat catcher Jody Miller following UA's 1991 NCAA softball title victory over UCLA. *Courtesy, University of Arizona Athletic Department.*

under the auspices of the AIAW). The Wildcats placed seventh in 1974 and returned to Omaha in 1975, placing eighth.

In 1977 new head coach Ginny Parrish led the team to new heights at the College World Series, placing second. Forced to play three games on the final day of the tournament, the dauntless Wildcats defeated defending champion Michigan State 2-1 and Northern Iowa 1-0 before losing to Northern Iowa 7-0 in the championship game.

In 1979 the Wildcats posted an impressive 44-15 record and won their first Intermountain Conference title with a 15-3 league mark, but finished a disappointing 13th in the College World Series. During the early 1980s, under former player and future athletic department administrator Kathleen "Rocky" LaRose (1980) and Paula Noel (1981-85) Arizona was competitive, but no longer could claim to be a nationally respected program.

Ironically, it was an ASU alumnus who would be responsible for returning UA softball to its former prominence. When he was hired in 1986, 30-year old Mike Candrea brought with him a winning reputation that he would quickly translate into victories for the Wildcat softball program. He had been a player at junior college power Central Arizona College and assistant coach on the CAC team that won the NJCAA (National Junior College Athletic Association) title in 1976. After earning bachelor's and master's degrees at ASU, he returned to CAC in 1981 as head softball coach and in five seasons took the school to three NJCAA tournaments and two national titles 1984 and 1985.

In his first season at Arizona, Candrea earned Pac-West Conference Co-Coach of the Year honors, improving the Wildcats from 17-16 in 1985 to a 27-13-1 record and a ranking as high as 11th during the season. In 1987 he was Pac-10 Co-Coach of the Year, leading Arizona to a 42-18 mark and its first ever NCAA Regional playoff berth.

In 1988, behind the strong arm of Teresa Cherry, who won a school-record 32 games, Arizona hosted and won the NCAA Mideast Regional in

In the 1920s and 1930s, riflery was extremely popular among UA women. Posing with their coach from the Military Department are coed shooters from the late 1920s. No doubt the sign behind them reflects the photographer's sense of humor. *Courtesy, University of Arizona Athletic Department.*

Tucson to earn its first berth in the Softball College World Series in Sunnyvale, California. The Cats won their first two games, 1-0 over Adelphi and 4-1 over Cal Poly-Pomona, before falling to eventual champion UCLA 5-0 and Fresno State 4-0 to tie for third. The team finished with a 54-18 record (a school record for wins), Cherry was a second-team All-American and freshman Julie Standering and senior Heidi Lievens earned all-tournament honors.

The following year, Arizona was 48-19 overall and duplicated its 1988 College World Series finish, placing third as UCLA won its fifth title in eight years. In 1990 with all but two regulars back, Candrea's squad was a strong favorite to end UCLA's dominance. However, the season ended on a sour note in Oklahoma City (where the Softball College World Series had been moved), as the Wildcats lost their first two games, failing to score a run in losses to Oklahoma State 3-0 and Fresno State 1-0. Senior outfielder Vivian Holm became the first UA player to be named a first-team All-American, and Julie Jones (2nd team) and Nicki Dennis (3rd) also garnered All-America honors.

Fittingly, Marguerite Chesney's nickname was "Miss Tennis." A dominant player in her youth and later a vigorous promoter of tournaments, she was the first woman to attend a meeting of the National Lawn Tennis Association and served as president of the Southwest Tennis Association. During her tenure, many outstanding women tennis players emerged from the UA campus. *Courtesy, Special Collections, University of Arizona Library.*

After three consecutive CWS trips and the disappointment of 1990, the 1991 UA softball team was not to be denied. On its way to a 56-16 record and the school's first national title, the team was led by iron-armed Debby Day, a junior transfer from Texas-Arlington. At Oklahoma City, she won three straight extra-inning shutout victories over Nevada-Las Vegas (13 innings), UCLA (9) and Long Beach State (8), all by 1-0 scores, to reach the final against three-time defending champion UCLA. This time the Wildcats prevailed, smashing the Bruins 5-1 in the championship game.

Day was the star of the series, winning four games while allowing one run and 15 hits in 32 innings. She was also 5-for-12 at the plate and headed the all-tournament team, which also included Julie Jones, Julie Standering and Kristin Gauthier. Standering, who would later earn a gold medal for the U.S. in the Pan American Games in Cuba, was named a first team All-American, while Jones and Day earned second- and third-team honors, respectively.

In 1992, after splitting the season series at home and away with UCLA to win its first Pac-10 title, Arizona returned to Oklahoma City to defend its national title, entering the College World Series with an impressive 55-5 record. Once, again matters were resolved by a Wildcat-Bruin showdown for the title.

This time, however, it would go to UCLA. The Bruins raced through the Series undefeated, giving up only one run, while Arizona had to battle its way through the losers bracket. After losing to Long Beach State 1-0 in their first game, the Wildcats took the measure of Kansas 1-0 in 17 innings, California 2-1 and Fresno State 1-0. In the cham-

Although extensive intercollegiate competition for women was still four decades away, UA coeds in the 1930s continued to explore available avenues of athletic expression. This UA women's bicycle club posed beside a road sign almost 20 miles from campus before beginning the return trek. *Courtesy, University of Arizona Athletic Department.*

Coaching Profile: Mike Candrea

When Candrea replaced Paula Noel at the UA in 1986, he was hired just as school started, on August 21, 1985. He didn't have time to do much about recruiting or scheduling. His first UA team played only four home games and had just 13 players on the roster. Yet he bettered the previous season's record by 10 victories.

In his six seasons at Arizona Candrea has led the Wildcats to five consecutive NCAA Regional appearances and four straight College World Series appearances. The 1991 season saw Arizona win its first women's NCAA team title, and in 1992 the Cats won the Pac-10 title and finished second at the NCAA tournament.

Candrea came to the University of Arizona after spending five years at Central Arizona Junior College where he compiled a winning percentage of .728 (185-69). He was named Junior College Coach of the Year in 1984 and 1985 after his team won consecutive national titles. In 1982 he coached Central Arizona to second place in the NJCAA.

Noted as one of the top hitting coaches in the nation, Candrea also has his team playing well in other areas. The pitching staff turned in team ERAs under 1.00 for the 1989-90-91 seasons. Defensively, the Wildcats have a fielding percentage of near .960 for those same three years.

But don't expect Candrea to be satisfied with past accomplishments. "I want to build a solid base here," he said, "so kids will grow up wanting to come to Arizona to play softball."

Mike Candrea has led the Wildcats to five consecutive NCAA regional appearances and four straight CWS appearances. ***Courtesy, University of Arizona Athletic Department.***

BEAR CANYON
ROAD

GREAT MOMENTS

Wildcat Softball Team Wins 1991 College World Series

Capturing the NCAA banner!
Courtesy, University of Arizona Athletic Department.

In many ways the 1991 Wildcat softball team represents all that is good about college athletics. Coach Mike Candrea raves about the team's qualities: unselfishness, dedication, enthusiasm and leadership. These are the same qualities that have rapidly made Work Recovery Inc. an international success. By its fifth year of operation, the company had doubled its annual sales and was in its ninth straight quarter of profitability. The Tucson-based company has installations of its diagnostic health care equipment in strategic locations across the United States as well as in Canada, Europe and Australia. The primary products for physical capacity assessment and work conditioning that Work Recovery manufactures are the Ergos Work Simulator and Transition Work Stations.

The UA softball team played its opening game of the College World Series a day late, but the Wildcats' pitcher Debby Day came through it just in time and defeated UNLV 1-0 in a 13-inning first game that was delayed 24 hours because of rain.

The Wildcats left 13 runners on base, but finally broke through when Kristin Gauthier led off the top of the 13th with a walk and was forced at second on a fielder's choice by Julie Jones. Suzie Lady's sacrifice bunt moved Jones to second. Jody Miller then came to the plate, the 15th time a Wildcat had a chance to drive in a runner in scoring position. This time Miller succeeded. She hit a single to right-center field, driving in Jones without a play. Day retired the side in order in the bottom of the inning.

In the second game of the doubleheader, Arizona beat top-ranked UCLA 1-0 in nine innings.

"That was a great ball game," UA coach Mike Candrea recalled. "We went to Oklahoma thinking that we were just not going to watch UCLA win again. And, obviously, we were not a bit intimidated."

For the second straight game, Julie Jones scored the winning run when she led off the bottom of the ninth with a sharp single up the middle. Suzie Lady walked on a 3-2 pitch and Jody Miller advanced both runners with a sacrifice bunt, bringing up Lisa Guise whose chopper over the Bruin third baseman, gave Jones time to cross the plate.

And then, in the fading daylight of Oklahoma City on May 26, the University of Arizona softball team turned the ASA Hall of Fame Stadium into its field of dreams. Facing UCLA again after the Bruins beat Long Beach 1-0, Arizona beat them 5-1 in the championship game, ending the Bruins' three-year dominance and giving the UA women its first NCAA team title.

It was a perfect day, UA coach Mike Candrea would later say, and Debby Day was nearly perfect. She threw a four-hitter, allowing a home run in the fourth. But Day was in control for most of the game, as she was for the series.

Again, the big hit came from Julie Jones. With two outs in the third and no score, she hit a triple that drove in two runs increasing UA's lead to 4-0 in the fourth and reached the final margin of 5-1 in the fifth.

Mike Candrea is a relentless recruiter and an uncanny evaluator of talent. He brought in the foundation for the UA's national championship—seniors Julie Jones, Suzie Lady, Julie Standering, Kristin Gauthier and Marcia Aguilar and junior pitcher Debby Day, with a bold and brash pledge. "I told each and every one of them that they would walk out of the University of Arizona as national champions."

In the postgame interview, Candrea grinned and said, "It hasn't sunk in. I keep pinching myself to make sure it's real."

But the sign on the door of his office in McKale Center tells all who pass that Candrea does, indeed, know it's real: "The Wildcats are national champions."

pionship game, a two-run homer off of Debby Day in the bottom of the seventh broke a scoreless tie, and the Bruins were NCAA champions for the eighth time in 11 years.

Arizona finished 58-7, a school record for both wins and winning percentage (.892) while UCLA was 54-2, its only losses coming at the hands of the Wildcats. Day, who also earned first-team All-America honors, freshman first-basemen Amy Chellevold, sophomore third-baseman Susie Duarte and sophomore pitcher Susie Parra were named to the all-tournament team.

> **QUOTABLES**
>
> "I've been a fan of the University of Arizona's sports teams since I was a freshman at the U of A in 1938. Their commitment to being the best in sports from baseball to water polo inspires alumni like me and keeps us coming back year after year to see some of the country's best college athletes perform. Since my graduation in 1942, I've stayed close to the university, and one of the big reasons I have is because of the Wildcats."
>
> ROBERT LESHER,
> *Lesher & Borodkin, Attorneys*

With one national title and five consecutive Softball College World Series appearances behind him, Candrea has brought softball to the pinnacle of women's team sports at the UA. And there is no indication that there will be anything less than continued success in the future.

VOLLEYBALL

Prior to Title IX and the formation of true varsity athletic programs for women at the UA in the 1970s, volleyball was one of the first women's sports to play an intercollegiate schedule against outside competition.

Beginning in 1966, Dr. Kathryn Russell became the sport's first full-fledged head coach, and the Wildcat setters and spikers played matches against four-year schools and junior colleges in Arizona and New Mexico. Nancy Trego, who also served four years as women's basketball coach (1975-78), served for two years, 1972 and 1973, while Russell was on sabbatical.

In 1974 Russell returned and led Arizona to its first 20-win season (20-5), including handing Intermountain Conference and AIAW Regional champion BYU its only defeat. Russell concluded

Senior shortstop Julie Standering, shown here in 1988, anchored Arizona's rock-solid defense during its 1991 championship season. She also batted leadoff for the Cats and exemplified a team noted for leadership and spirit in addition to talent. Standering was named first team All America prior to the NCAA College World Series. *Courtesy, University of Arizona Athletic Department.*

Coaching Profile: Joan Bonvicini

Joan Bonvicini is one of the most successful collegiate basketball coaches in the sport's history. She compiled a record of 325-71 during her tenure at Long Beach State from 1979-91 and became the head coach of UA women's basketball beginning with the 1991-92 season.

Bonvicini coached Long Beach to all 10 NCAA women's basketball tournaments. The 49ers advanced to the women's Final Four in 1987 and 1988. Long Beach State is one of only five colleges to play in all 10 NCAA tournaments.

"I've had great success at Long Beach State and it was a difficult decision to leave, but after meeting with the players and the University of Arizona athletic department staff, my decision was very easy...I'm ready for a change."

Bonvicini received a bachelor of arts degree from Southern Connecticut State in 1975 where she was an outstanding guard. She led her team to third and fourth place finishes in the 1974 and 1975 AIAW national championships. Bonvicini was the region 1-A Most Valuable Player and received All-America Honorable Mention honors in 1975. She was a finalist as a player on the 1976 U.S. Olympic team.

Bonvicini believes the Wildcats can be among the elite in women's college basketball and she's determined to handle the program accordingly. She wants the Ladycats to lead the Pac-10 in attendance within three years and lead the nation within five.

As a result there are already a lot of people excited about women's basketball in Tucson.

Joan Bonvicini brings an outstanding coaching career to the University of Arizona. *Courtesy, University of Arizona Athletic Department.*

her coaching career in 1976 with a 22-6 record and Arizona's first appearance in the AIAW National Championship, where the Wildcats tied for 16th in a field of 32.

The history of Wildcat volleyball for the next 15 years can be summed up in two words: Rosie Wegrich. A standout player in her own right at San Diego State and in the International Volleyball Association (a very popular pro league in the 1970s that fea-

In 1991 Anika Sorenstam led the Wildcats to a third-place team finish. She successfully defended the NCAA crown won by Suasan Slaughter, whose out-of-the-pack triumph in the 1990 NCAA women's golf championship was the first national title for a UA golfer. A conflict with coach Kim Haddow the following year prompted Slaughter to leave school and hit the tour. *Courtesy, University of Arizona Athletic Department.*

In 1985 UA's Katrena Johnson (waving) won the NCAA high jump championship—and teammates Maryse Ewanje-Epee and Camille Harding (to her immediate left) finished second and third, respectively. This was the first and only time that three athletes from the same school swept the top three places in an NCAA championship. *Courtesy, University of Arizona Athletic Department.*

tured four-man, two-woman teams), Wegrich became head coach at the UA in 1977, after two seasons at the University of Minnesota.

Under her guidance, the Wildcat volleyball program continued to excel on the conference and regional level and soon had become a national contender. Her first team in 1977 won the Intermountain Regional tournament and tied for ninth in the AIAW Championship. The 1978 team was 28-15-3 (still the school record for most victories), won the school's only conference title, going 11-1 in league play and tied for 13th in the AIAW tourney.

Arizona's switch from the Intermountain Conference to the Western Collegiate Athletic Association (WCAA) in 1979 was a major step up in level of competition, as the Wildcats would now face the perennial West Coast national powers on a regular basis.

Playing anywhere else in the country or in any conference but the WCAA/Pac-West or Pac-10, Wildcat volleyball would have been one of the dominant programs in its league and region. Under Wegrich, the UA was one of just nine schools that qualified for the NCAA Championship each of the first nine years of the tournament (1981-89). However, the California schools were so dominant, first in the WCAA/Pac-West and then the Pac-10, that the Wildcats were never able to break into the first division in either league or to advance past the second round in NCAA tournament play.

During the WCAA/Pac-West era (1981-85), league schools won two NCAA titles and at least two teams—three in 1981 and 1985—made the Final Four every year. Since the Pac-10 began women's competition in 1986, the league twice has had seven teams awarded NCAA postseason tournament berths, and UCLA or Stanford

COACHING PROFILE: DAVID RUBIO

Following the departure of UA head coach Rosie Wegrich after the 1991 season, David Rubio arrived to assume the leadership of Wildcat volleyball, bringing with him an eye-popping record of success.

In 1987 Rubio inherited a Cal State Bakersfield Roadrunner team that finished the 1986 season with a 6-23 record and 1-11 California Collegiate Athletic Conference record. Within two years he provided Bakersfield with the winningest record in school history and its first winning record in the CCAC. That was just for starters. In 1989 his team reached the pinnacle of the volleyball world by claiming the NCAA Division II national championship. In 1990 the Roadrunners won a school-record 31 matches and in 1991 the team won its first CCAC title. His modest five-year totals: one national championship, one CCAC championship, one CCAC Coach of the Year award, one ASICS Tiger Coach of the Year award, three "Elite Eight" appearances, four playoff appearances, seven All-Americans, an overall record of 120-65 and post-season winning percentage of .727.

The Wildcats have landed another winner.

Rubio entered the 1992 season with a commitment to organization, discipline and hard work. He has a strong group of returning letter winners and a handful of highly touted recruits.

DAVID RUBIO
Courtesy, University of Arizona Athletic Department.

has been in the Final Four every year, the Bruins winning in 1990 and 1991.

Win or lose, volleyball has regularly drawn the most spectator support of any UA women's team. Until 1983 all home matches were held before overflow crowds in the Gittings Building Gym. Since moving to McKale Center in 1983, the UA has hosted NCAA Championship First Round matches in 1983, 1985 and 1989. In 1989 total season attendance for the season, with a

During her four years at Arizona, Melissa "Missy" McLinden shattered UA's records for kills and blocks, and in 1985, her senior season, she became Arizona's first first-team All-American in volleyball. She went on to become a member of the 1988 U.S. Olympic team. *Photo: Tom Bingham. Courtesy, University Photo Center.*

In 1983, team captain Anita Moss became the first UA Wildcat to earn All America distinction in volleyball. Following her senior season she was selected for the U.S. World University games team and later went on to a professional volleyball career in Europe. *Courtesy, University of Arizona Athletic Department.*

Arizona diving and swimming champion Nancy Kinney MacBeth answered her athletic calling—even if it took her about 30 years to do it. After graduating in 1950 and raising seven children, she returned to competitive swimming in the late 1970s and became national and world champion at the masters and senior levels. At the present, she is still competing—and winning. *Courtesy, University of Arizona Athletic Department.*

victory over Oregon in the NCAA playoff, averaged 1,066 per match, including an all-time record of 2,329 against UCLA.

In her 15 years at Arizona, Wegrich had only three losing seasons, took her teams into post-season AIAW or NCAA play 12 times and had a career record of 258-229-9.

Individual standouts during the Wegrich era included the school's three All-Americans: Anita Moss in 1982 and 1983; Caren Kemner, 1984, and Melissa "Missy" McLinden, 1985; two-time All-Pac-10 selection Terry Lauchner, 1987-88, and Canadian national team member Mary Linton. Kemner and McLinden went on to star on the U.S. National Team and both played in the 1988 Olympics. Kemner, considered by many experts as the top women's player in the world, was the captain of the 1992 U.S. Olympic team in Barcelona, Spain.

QUOTABLES

"**V**ision Quest has supported the U of A's sports programs for a number of years. Several of our employees are graduates of or former athletes at the U of A, and all of them are Wildcat fanatics. Here's hoping all the great U of A teams 'Bear Down' for many winning years to come."

STEVE ROGERS,
President,
Vision Quest

A new era in UA volleyball began in the fall of 1992.

Following the 1991 season, in which the Wildcat volleyballers struggled to their poorest record ever, 4-26 and failed to win a single Pac-10 match, Wegrich's contract was not renewed. Replacing her was 32-year old David Rubio, who had a five-year record of 121-65 at Cal State-Bakersfield and won the NCAA Division II title in 1989.

Several times AIAW and NCAA champion in the shotput and discus in the early 1980s, Meg Ritchie was All-America for four years, competed in two Olympic games and set records at Arizona that seem unlikely to be broken for a long, long time. Following her retirement she became UA strength coach, the first woman selected for such a position at a major university. *Photo: Mike Stoklos.*

ARIZONA
31
asics

Basketball

With just four winning seasons since intercollegiate competition began in 1972-73, there has been a lot of pain and little glory for women's basketball at the University of Arizona. While the men's program flourished, winning conference titles and reaching national prominence under Fred Snowden and Lute Olson during the 1970s and 1980s, Arizona's women hoopsters have traveled a long and winding road with countless potholes and many breakdowns along the way.

Simply put, no other sport at UA, men's or women's, has had as little success on the conference or national level as women's basketball; it is the only sport that has never been nationally ranked or qualified for post-season play, either in the AIAW or NCAA. Before its elevation to true varsity status in 1975-76, the Ladycats enjoyed limited success against regional opposition, posting consecutive records of 8-4, 11-4 and 12-4 from 1972-73 to 1974-75. But that would be the last winning season until 1985-86.

In the intervening 10 years, under head coaches Nancy Trego, Lori Woodman and Judy LeWinter, the record was 65-170, a decade-long percentage of just .277.

In the 1985-86 season Wendy Larry, a former player and top assistant at Old Dominion, one of the country's most successful women's programs, led the Ladycats to their first winning record in 11 years—19-9 overall and a tie for second in the short-lived Pac-West Conference. After an 11-18 mark the following season, and UA's first in Pac-10 play, Larry took the top job at her alma mater, and her assistant,

Softball No Hitters

Fast-pitch softball pitchers throw from a flat pitcher's circle 43 feet from home plate. Balls travel 63 to 67 m.p.h., or the equivalent of a 90 m.p.h. fastball in baseball. Unlike a baseball, a softball can break on four planes, which adds the rising ball to a pitcher's repertoire.

These pitchers hurled no-hitters:

Pitcher Date	Opponent
Tonja Anderson	
4/17/77	Northern Arizona
5/28/77	Arizona State
Sandy Miramontes	
4/17/82	Southern California
Sheryl Kempkes	
3/11/83	San Diego State
Pam Stone	
3/06/84	UC-Santa Barbara
Sandy Miramontes	
5/04/84	Oregon
Teresa Cherry	
3/07/87	Central Michigan
Lisa Bautista	
2/25/88	Oklahoma (5 innings)
Teresa Cherry	
3/26/87	Fresno State
Leslie VanOver	
3/12/88	Oregon State
3/24/88	San Francisco
Doreen Juarez	
5/06/89	California
Ginnie Scheller	
2/24/90	UC-Santa Barbara
Doreen Juarez	
4/13/90	Oregon State
Julie Jones	
4/21/90	California
Debby Day	
2/14/91	Pacific (5 innings)
2/22/91	UNLV
Susie Parra	
2/14/91	UC-Santa Barbara
Julie Jones	
3/22/91	Colorado State
Debby Day	
3/22/91	Oregon State
Susie Parra	
4/05/91	St. Mary's (5 innings)
Debby Day	
4/05/91	St. Mary's
Susie Parra	
4/11/92	Oregon State
Debby Day	
4/24/92	Oregon State
4/25/92	Oregon

Margo Clark, a scorer-rebounder, has given a major boost to Coach Joan Bonvicini's rebuilding of the U of A women's basketball program. Clark was named First Team All Pac-10 in 1991-92. *Courtesy , Robert F. Walker, University Photo Center.*

former Rutgers All-American June Olkowski, was named to succeed her.

One of the youngest head coaches in the country at age 27, Olkowski struggled through four losing seasons, going 34-82 overall (.293) and never managing better than a tie for eighth in the Pac-10. In 1990-91, after the Ladycats were 6-25 (the most losses in school history) and lost 19 of their final 20 games to finish 1-71 and in last place in the Pac-10, Olkowski's contract was not renewed and Athletic Director Cedric Dempsey made a bold step to raise the level of Arizona's women's basketball to that of the rest of the school's teams.

Not unlike his inspired hiring of Lute Olson in 1984, Dempsey sought out and hired one of the brightest young coaching talents in the country in Joan Bonvicini—the nation's winningest female NCAA Division I head coach. In 12 seasons at Long Beach State, the 37-year old Connecticut native posted a winning percentage of .821 (325-71). She was NCAA Coach of the Year in 1981, won 10 conference titles, took teams to NCAA post-season play 10 times, reaching the Final Four twice and regional final three times, and never won fewer than 24 games in a season.

Upon hiring Bonvicini, Dempsey noted that "with the increased national exposure and prominence being given to women's basketball, it is critical we bring basketball up to the level of our other men's and women's sports. We're confident that Joan Bonvicini is the one to do that."

Bonvicini is confident that she can get the job done, saying: "We will challenge for the Pac-10 title and be in the NCAAs. Maybe not this season, maybe not next, but soon. This town is big enough for two basketball teams to be successful. The local community has shown that it will support a winner, and that's what I intend to put on the court."

Hopefully, with Bonvicini in the driver's seat, the narrow, bumpy road that UA women's basketball has traveled in its first 20 years will finally join the highly successful men's program on a fast and wide highway to a winning record, strong community support, and national prominence.

NOTABLES

Arizona's Southwest Championship in 1914 inspired the students to construct a huge, white-washed "A" on Sentinel Peak. This popular project was commemorated in a special inscribed photograph. *Courtesy: University of Arizona Athletic Department.*

Freshman Tanya Hughes accomplished a unique "double" in 1991, winning both the indoor and outdoor NCAA women's high jump championships. Her winning jumps were 6' 2" indoors and 6 ' 4 1/4" outdoors. *Photo: Tony Duffy/Allsport. Courtesy, University of Arizona Athletic Department.*

105

University of Arizona Women's Team Sports Statistical Highlights

Women's Basketball

Season's Records

Year	Coach	W-L	Conference@ W-L	Pl.
1972-73	Lois Sheldahl	7-4		
1973-74	Lois Sheldahl	11-4		
1974-75	Nancy Trego	12-4	9-2	2T
1975-76	Nancy Trego	6-8	6-7	
1976-77	Nancy Trego	3-13	3-11	
1977-78	Nancy Trego	4-14	3-10	
1978-79	Lori Woodman	6-18	5-8	8T
1979-80	Lori Woodman	9-17	1-11	7
1980-81	Judy LeWinter	2-21	1-11	7
1981-82	Judy LeWinter	10-21	0-12	7
1982-83	Judy LeWinter	10-17	2-17	7T
1983-84	Judy LeWinter	8-20	1-13	7T
1984-85	Judy LeWinter	7-21	1-13	8
1985-86	Wendy Larry	19-9	4-4	2T
1986-87	Wendy Larry	11-18	4-14	8T
1987-88	June Olkowski	5-23	2-16	10
1988-89	June Olkowski	11-17	6-12	8T
1989-90	June Olkowski	12-17	5-13	8T
1990-91	June Olkowski	6-25	1-17	10
1991-92	Joan Bonvicini	9-19	3-15	9T

@-Intermountain Athletic Conference, 1974-79; Western Collegiate Athletic Association, 1979-85; Pac-West Conference, 1985-86; Pacific 10 Conference, 1986-present

Women's Basketball Top Ten (Career)

Points		
1315	Timi Brown	1990-91
1299	Dana Patterson	1984-88
1264	Kirsten Smith	1982-86
1144	Yolanda Turner	1983-87
960	Miroslava Acosta	1985-87
925	Regina Grennan	1986-90
883	Melissa Handley	1987
805	Leslie Martin	1980-83
783	Pam Roberts	1978-82
731	Margo Clark	1990-92

Women's Volleyball

Season's Records

Year	Coach	W-L	Conference@ W-L	Pl.
1966	Kathryn Russell	*Records not available*		
1967	Kathryn Russell	*Records not available*		
1968	Kathryn Russell	*Records not available*		
1969	Kathryn Russell	*Records not available*		
1970	Kathryn Russell	*Records not available*		
1971	Kathryn Russell	*Records not available*		
1972	Nancy Trego	*Records not available*		
1973	Nancy Trego	*Records not available*		
1974	Kathryn Russell	20-5		
1975	Kathryn Russell	16-11	12-1	2
1976	Kathryn Russell	22-6	10-2	2
1977	Rosie Wegrich	17-12-2	14-8	2
1978	Rosie Wegrich	28-15-3	11-1	1
1979	Rosie Wegrich	8-17-2	2-10	6
1980	Rosie Wegrich	20-17	5-7	4
1981	Rosie Wegrich	22-18-2	5-7	4
1982	Rosie Wegrich	22-16	5-9	6
1983	Rosie Wegrich	17-15	7-7	5
1984	Rosie Wegrich	16-12	6-8	5
1985	Rosie Wegrich	17-13	1-7	5
1986	Rosie Wegrich	14-15	9-9	6
1987	Rosie Wegrich	18-13	9-9	6
1988	Rosie Wegrich	19-14	9-9	5
1989	Rosie Wegrich	18-13	8-10	6
1990	Rosie Wegrich	18-13	8-10	6T
1991	Rosie Wegrich	4-24	0-18	10
1992	David Rubio	4-26	0-18	10
Total		**320-275-9**		

@-Intermountain Athletic Conference, 1975-78; Western Collegiate Athletic Conference, 1979-84; Pac-West Conference, 1985; Pacific 10 Conference, 1986-present

Women's Volleyball Season and Career Leaders

Kills			
Season	520	Terry Lauchner	1988
Career	1239	Melissa McLinden	1982-85

Assists (Assists cumulative from 1978, 1983-89 only)			
Season	1363	Mary Linton	1989
Career	2954	Mary Linton	1986-89

Solo Blocks			
Season	55	Cindy Andrews	1978
Career	118	Melissa McLinden	1982-85

Assisted Blocks			
Season	182	Kelly Waage	1988
Career	436	Kelly Waage	1986-89

Service Aces			
Season	55	Brooke Saunders	1984
Career	123	Brooke Saunders	1981-84

Digs (Digs cumulative from 1978, 1983-89 only)			
Season	401	Terry Lauchner	1988
Career	1155	Lindsey Hahn	1986-89

University of Arizona Women's Team Sports Statistical Highlights

Women's Softball Individual Hitting Records

Batting Average, Season (100 or more at bats)

	AB	H	AVG.	Year
Gail Davenport	121	50	.413	1977
Nicki Dennis	207	76	.367	1989
Regina Rawson	110	40	.364	1975
Dee Dinota	111	40	.360	1981
Mary Cassidy	124	43	.343	1981
Jamie Heggen	198	67	.338	1992
Jamie Heggen	179	59	.330	1991
Stacy Engel	179	59	.330	1987
Vivian Holm	219	72	.329	1990
Kristin Gauthier	215	70	.326	1990
Stacy Engel	114	37	.325	1986
Nicki Dennis	174	56	.322	1990

Batting Average, Career (225 or more at bats)

	AB	H	AVG.	Year
Nicki Dennis	381	132	.346	1989-90
Gail Davenport	468	149	.318	1976-79
Kristin Gauthier	547	171	.313	1988-90
Julie Jones	412	123	.299	1989-90
Vivian Holm	816	241	.295	1987-90
Rocky LaRose	235	68	.289	1978-79
Dee Dinota	477	138	.289	1981-84
Julie Winklepleck	303	86	.271	1979-81
Regina Rawson	524	145	.278	1979-82
Stacy Engel	695	186	.268	1986-89

Home Runs, Season

Nicki Dennis	7	1989
Jamie Wheat	4	1987
Jamie Wheat	4	1988
Julie Winklepleck	4	1979
Julie Winklepleck	4	1981
Barb Garcia	3	1978-80
Regina Rawson	3	1980
Gail Davenport	3	1976-79
Rocky LaRose	3	1978
Norma Gallego	3	1976
Tonya Adreon	3	1976

Home Runs, Career

Barb Garcia	9	1978-81
Gail Davenport	8	1976-79
Nicki Dennis	8	1989-90
Jamie Wheat	8	1984-88
Dee Dinota	5	1981-84
Regina Rawson	4	1979-82
Julie Winklepleck	4	1979-81
Terry Haggerty	4	1975-79

Softball Individual Pitching Records

Wins, Season

Debby Day	32	1992
Teresa Cherry	32	1988
Debby Day	30	1991
Susie Parra	26	1992
Lisa Bautista	25	1989
Kathi Rosenbery	25	1979
Julie Jones	21	1990
Teresa Cherry	19	1987
Jo Longanecker	18	1979
Lisa Bautista	18	1987
Doreen Juarez	17	1990
Jo Longanecker	15	1980
Teresa Cherry	13	1986
Ginnie Scheller	13	1989

Wins, Career

Teresa Cherry	71	85-88
Lisa Bautista	55	86-89
Jo Longanecker	46	79-82
Ginnie Scheller	38	87-90
Sheryl Kempkes	32	86-86
Kathi Rosenberry	29	79-80
Pam Stone	29	82-84
Doreen Juarez	27	89-90
Julie Jones	21	89-90
Sandy Miramontes	19	82-84

Strikeouts, Career

Pam Stone	343	82-84
Lisa Bautista	263	86-89
Jo Longanecker	253	79-82
Teresa Cherry	220	85-88
Ginnie Scheller	155	87-90
Doreen Juarez	140	89-90
Sheryle Kempkes	137	83-86
Kathi Rosenberry	115	79-80
Sandy Miramontes	98	82-84
Julie Jones	93	89-90

While basketball, football and baseball generated most of the media and fan attention during the decade of the '80s, University of Arizona athletes in other sports made perhaps the biggest contribution to the development of what has become one of the nation's top-ranked all-around collegiate athletic programs.

NCAA champions, Olympic medalists, numerous All-Americans and members of U.S. national teams in international competition have carried the name of the university to the far corners

At the 1991 NCAA swimming and diving championships, Arizona's Crissy Ahmann-Leighton won the 100-yard butterfly and became only the second UA woman to win an NCAA swimming title. Her time of 52.36 was a new NCAA, American and U.S. Open record. She also finished 3rd in the 50-yard and 100-yard freestyle events. *Photo: Jon Alquist. Arizona Alumni Association.*

PERSONAL BEST

of the nation and the world.

The 1991-92 school year, according to the annual national all-sports ranking published in *USA Today*, the combined men's and women's intercollegiate program at the UA was the third best in the country. The women's program ranked third, while the men's came in fifth. Of the school's 17 varsity sports , six of eight men's and seven of nine women's, ranked in the top 20 and advanced to postseason competition.

This earliest known photograph of athletic competition at the university was taken by Tucson pioneer businessman and civic leader Sam Mansfeld on February 22, 1901. The occasion was a track-and-field meet between UA and a group of Tucson athletes, and the photo taken was of the finish of the 100 yard dash, won by M.B. "Bing" Morse in 10 2/5 seconds. *Courtesy, University of Arizona Athletic Department.*

These rankings point out the rise in prominence of women's programs. This began with incorporation into the NCAA championship structure in 1981-82. Prior to that, women's programs had come under the jurisdiction of the Association of Intercollegiate Athletics for Women (AIAW).

Since beginning varsity competition in the early 1970s, UA women have competed in four conferences, the Intermountain until 1979, the Western Collegiate Athletic Association (WCAA), 1979-85, the short-lived Pac-West in 1985-86, and now the Pac-10, which began full-scale women's competition in nine sports in 1986-87.

While most non-revenue sports at the UA have flourished, financial pressure to operate a balanced and competitive program has resulted in the demise of wrestling, men's gymnastics, and synchronized swimming (a non-NCAA sport), which won three national titles in the 1980s and developed 1984 Olympic gold medalists Tracie Ruiz and Candy Costie. Also gone from the program are the team sports of field hockey and water polo.

MEN'S AND WOMEN'S TRACK AND FIELD

The first recorded, organized athletic competition at the University of Arizona was in the sport of track and field. In 1897, the first meet

At this 1916 track meet Asa Porter won the long jump (known as the "broad jump" at the time) with a leap of 21' 2 1/2 ", a new school and meet record. *Courtesy, The Asa Porter Family.*

consisting of 12 events, was held with the local town team. Thereafter, competition during the territorial period was pretty much impromptu, although a dual meet was held in 1904 with the Bisbee YMCA. The first collegiate meet took place in 1908 against the Tempe Normal School (Arizona State), and soon after that UA athletes began competing in various relay meets and invitationals on the West Coast and in Texas.

Regional competition began in 1916 when the first Southwestern Intercollegiate Meet (including schools in Arizona, New Mexico and west Texas) was held on May 6 at the University's new athletic field located behind the recently completed College of Agriculture building. The sport continued to improve its level of competition following World War I, as UA athletes entered major meets in the region and dual meets were regularly held with such schools as San Diego State, UCLA and traditional rivals Arizona State and New Mexico.

The most memorable accomplishment by a UA athlete during the early days of the sport occurred in 1927, when Wildcat track captain John Scott upset Olympic champion Charlie Paddock in an exhibition 220-yard dash at the Greenway Meet at the state fairgrounds in Phoenix. Keeping his pre-meet promise to retire if he beat Paddock, Scott promptly retired.

The first individual Arizona athletes to gain national prominence were hurdler Clyde Blanchard and javelin thrower Clarence "Bud" Sample. Blanchard tied the Pacific AAU record, narrowly missed earning a berth on the 1928 Olympic team in the 400-meter hurdles and placed third in the 1932 NCAA meet. Sample was the UA's first ever NCAA point-scorer in any sport, placing second in the javelin in

At the 1916 Southwest Track and Field Championships in Tucson, Arizona's Asa Porter destroyed the field in the 220-yard dash, winning in 23 1/5 seconds, a new UA record. *Courtesy, The Asa Porter Family.*

1932 and 1933. His 1933 throw of 211-4 stood as the school record until 1962.

Under coaches Walter Davis, Tex Oliver and F. T. "Limey" Gibbings, Arizona dominated track and field during the early years of the Border Conference, winning consecutive team titles from 1932 through 1946. During the later years of the league, the UA and Arizona State were the only conference schools with full-fledged programs. Following WWII, ASU dominated the BC and the Wildcats, winning eight of nine league titles between 1947-55.

Former Wildcat football and track star Carl Cooper became head coach in 1952, upsetting ASU for the conference title that year, and winning four of the final six BC meets. Cooper also brought the program to national prominence, developing 12 All-Americans, the UA's first NCAA champion (long jumper Gayle Hopkins in 1964), three Olympians and two American record holders.

In the center of this photo of the 1928-29 UA swim team is a promising freshman freestyler, Barry Goldwater. Young Goldwater left the university after his freshman year to return to Phoenix and help run the family business. *Courtesy, Special Collections, University of Arizona Library.*

His top team finishes in the NCAA Championships included a ninth in 1961, tenth in 1964 and eleventh in 1960 and 1966.

Top performers under Cooper included 1955 NCAA long-jump runner-up Mal Andrews; four-time Olympian and American record-holder in several events George Young, who earned a bronze medal in the steeplechase in 1968; Hopkins, a 1964 Olympic long jump finalist; 1968 silver-medal high jumper Ed Caruthers; and 1965 NCAA javelin champion John Tushaus, who broke the American record with a throw of 284 feet in 1966.

In 1970 Cooper left the UA to become executive director of the U.S. Track and Field Federation, and was replaced by Willie Williams, a former star sprinter at San Jose State. Williams was also the first black head coach at a major NCAA institution. Williams did a good job of keeping UA track and field in the national spotlight, producing 25 All-Americans and such standouts as U.S. national team members Larry Brown and Wardell Gilbreath in the sprints, 1976 Olympic distance runner Ed Mendoza, high jumper James Frazier and decathlete Steve Jacobs. His best NCAA finish was 11th in 1979 and his teams were ranked in the national dual-meet rankings top 20 seven times.

Williams served as a coach on several U.S. national teams and was named to the 1980 U.S. Olympic team coaching staff. In 1981 the UA track and field program took a giant step forward with the completion of the Rincon Vista track facility (later to be named Roy P. Drachman Stadium) at 15th St. and Plumer Ave., about a mile southeast of the main campus. The nine-lane Tartan surface track was a dream come true for Williams, who had been promised a new facility when he was hired, and a quantum improvement over the outdated and inadequate track in Arizona Stadium, which had been home to UA track meets since 1929.

Arizona's 118-pound Dale Brumit was the university's first and only three-time All-America wrestler. Also three times WAC champion, Brumit was twice named the WAC's outstanding wrestler. *Courtesy, University of Arizona Athletic Department.*

However, Williams would not live to see the fruition of his dream. For reasons still not fully understood today, on January 14, 1982, he was found dead at the track of a self-inflicted gunshot wound. Williams' death shocked the university community, but out of the tragedy would come triumph for UA track and field during the 1980s.

At the 1969 NCAA wrestling championships, UA's Gary Rushing finished third, but with gold-medal courage. Seriously ill a week before, he could not train and had to move into a heavier weight class. During the tournament he also suffered a serious leg injury but kept competing. In the match for third place he was rendered unconscious by an illegal hold; after being revived, he wrestled again and won. Twice WAC champion, Rushing was 1969 WAC wrestler of the year and All-America. *Courtesy, University of Arizona Athletic Department.*

Primarily responsible for this "golden" era of track and field at the UA were two unrelated head coaches with the same last name, Dave and Chris Murray. Dave, who succeeded Williams in 1982, is a 1964 UA graduate and former school-record holder in the 440-yard dash. In 1968 he succeeded Carl Cooper as head cross country coach and had served as assistant track coach under Williams until his death. His 1984 team was the finest in school history, finishing sixth in the NCAA Championships and second in the annual dual meet rankings compiled by *Track & Field News.*

In addition to four top-20 NCAA meet finishes, including four individual national champions, the Wildcat men have been ranked in the top 20 as a dual-meet team (five times in the top 10) every year since 1981.

In 1982 Vance Johnson became the UA's first NCAA individual men's titlist since 1965, winning the long jump with a still-standing school record of 26-9 ¼ Following him to the victory stand during the decade and into the 1990s have been Matt Giusto and Marc Davis, who won back-to-back 5,000-meter titles in 1988 and 1989, 1989 decathlon champion Derek Huff and Davis again in 1992 when he won the 3,000-meter steeplechase, becoming the first ever to win NCAA titles in the 5,000 and steeple.

The other half of the unrelated Murray duo of head coaches, Chris, came to Tucson in 1980 and almost overnight transformed the UA women's track from a virtual club program to a national power. Women's track and field had been given varsity status in 1977 but had received very little support or impetus until Murray came on the scene. During that decade Murray's teams amassed six outdoor and four indoor NCAA top 10 finishes and were in the top 10 in the dual meet rankings six times.

No other sport in UA history has produced more national champions, 15 AIAW and NCAA individual titles having been won by Wildcat women. Nearly half of those were claimed by two-time British Olympian Meg Ritchie, who won seven collegiate crowns. Her school records of 62-3 ¼ in the shot put and 221-5 in the discus, set in 1983 and 1981, respectively, still stand as the collegiate records. Another Olympian of the period was distance standout Joan Hansen, who set a world indoor two-mile record and was a finalist in the famous Mary Decker-Zola Budd 3,000-meter race at the 1984 Olympics in Los Angeles.

Arizona's other collegiate champions during the period include

Derek Huff's 7,629 points in the decathlon at the 1989 Pac-10 track and field championships were good enough for victory. At the ensuing NCAA championships, Huff upped his point total to 8,020 in the grueling event and became national champion, bettering by 284 the previous record of UA's Steve Jacobs, who was runner-up ten years earlier. *Photo: Brice Samuel. University of Arizona Athletic Department.*

In 1965 John Tushaus became the second UA Wildcat to capture an NCAA individual title when he won the javelin event. A year later Tushaus, a two-time WAC champion, broke both the American and NCAA records with a throw of 284 feet. *Courtesy, University of Arizona Athletic Department.*

Ritchie protégé Carla Garrett, winner of three shot put and discus titles, indoors and out in 1989; double high jump medalist Katrena Johnson who led an unprecedented 1-2-3 Arizona sweep of the event at the 1985 NCAA outdoor meet; AIAW 400-meter hurdles champ Robin Marks; 1982 NCAA indoor high jump winner Charmaine Gale; and 1984 NCAA indoor 400 meter titlist Ruth Waithera Nganga, a finalist for Kenya at the Los Angeles Olympics.

While at the UA, 20 of Chris Murray's athletes won 60 All-America awards in track and field. Chris Murray left the program following the 1990 season and in June of that year both men's and women's programs were consolidated under Dave Murray.

No better tribute could be paid to the accomplishments of University of Arizona track and field than the fact that 17 current or former Wildcats qualified to compete in the 1992 U.S. Olympic Trials in New Orleans—and six earned trips to Barcelona. Only two other schools, UCLA and Tennessee, provided more talent for the U.S. men's and women's Olympic track teams.

Winning their events at the trials were Sandra Farmer-Patrick, who competed at the UA in 1982, in the 400-meter hurdles, Donna Mayhew in the javelin, and sophomore high jumper Tanya Hughes. Hughes set a collegiate record of 6-5 ½ in winning the 1992 Pac-10 title and has won back-to-back NCAA outdoor championships, plus an NCAA indoor title in 1990. Also making the U.S. team were Michael Bates in the 200 meters, Carla

Arizona's first national champion in track and field was multi-talented jumper Gayle Hopkins, who won the NCAA long jump championship in 1964. He represented the U.S. at the 1964 Olympic Games in Tokyo. At present Dr. Gayle Hopkins is UA's Assistant Director of Athletics for Student-Athletic Services. *Courtesy, University of Arizona Athletic Department.*

ARIZONA

Garrett in the discus and Aaron Ramirez in the 10,000 meters.

MEN'S AND WOMEN'S CROSS COUNTRY

Cross country seems to have begun at the University of Arizona in 1915 when no track was available due to the construction of the new College of Agriculture building. A trophy was offered by a Mr. Brannen, and the UA harriers outran teams from Tucson High and the Tucson Indian School.

QUOTABLES

"Early in 1949, after I had won the 440-yard intramural championship, 'Pop' McKale asked me to go out for the track team. He made me feel ten feet tall. Three years later, I had won three varsity letters, honed competitive skills, and made many lifetime friends—including coach 'Limey' Gibbings, whose rough, tough, cigar-smoking facade hid a warm, caring heart."

S. JACK MCDUFF,
S. Jack McDuff & Associates, Inc.

Although a new track was available the next year, the Brannen Trophy race was run through 1919, and some form of cross country competition continued through the next several decades. On November 29, 1929, the UA team defeated runners from Arizona State, 15-21, with the race finishing in Arizona Stadium at halftime of the Arizona-Whittier football game.

Arizona racked up back-to-back victories in the men's 5,000 meter run at the NCAA championships when Marc Davis won in 1989. Fellow Wildcat Matt Giusto won the previous year. Davis holds the UA school record in the event by almost twelve seconds. *Photo: Robert F. Walker. University Photo Center.*

Credit for the establishment of cross country as true intercollegiate sport goes to Carl Cooper, who became head track-and-field coach in 1952. That fall he began a series of annual dual meets against Arizona State and within a few years the team began competing in invitationals, future Olympian George Young winning the Aztec Invitational in San Diego in 1957. In 1958 the sport achieved varsity status and in 1962 the first official team title to be awarded in the newly formed Western Athletic Conference was won by Arizona's cross country team.

Dave Murray replaced Cooper in 1968 and in 1972 the Wildcats qualified for their first NCAA Championship, placing 20th. The following year

Twin sisters, Joy and Joan Hansen, shown posing here in 1981 with miler Steve Scott for the cover of *Runner's World* magazine. At the University of Arizona, both were cross country All-Americans and conference champions. Joan was All-America in track also and was a member of the 1984 U.S. Olympic team in the 3,000 meter run. Joy was the U.S. national champion in the modern pentathlon and became a world-class triathlete. *Photo: David Madison.* Runner's World *magazine.*

G R E A T M O M E N T S

George DiCarlo Went the Distance for Olympic Gold and Silver

George DiCarlo

Because of its limited menu of exceptional items, the Tucson Cork has been a Tucson tradition for more than three decades. Restaurant owners William G. and Delores D. Hillenbrand have also gone the distance with University of Arizona athletics. Thanks to their timely and substantial gift, the recently remodeled Hillenbrand Aquatic Center now provides expanded and updated facilities to UA swimmers. The generosity of the Hillenbrands and the Tucson Cork towards Wildcat swimmers is the

William G. Hillenbrand

Like most outstanding swimmers, George DiCarlo began with United States Swimming age-group programs as a boy and progressed through junior-national and senior-national competition. By the time UA swim coach Dick Jochums saw George place eighth in the 1979 Seventeen Meet of Champions in Mission Viejo, California he had already garnered some impressive swimming credentials. But what most impressed Jochums was DiCarlo's work ethic. While not the most physically gifted swimmer, DiCarlo was a "blue collar swimmer" because he worked so hard.

"I didn't dive into the UA program with a lot of God-given talent, so I had to train really hard to accomplish what I wanted," says DiCarlo. He made All-America his first college season, and in the World Games U.S. trials the following summer, a victory and career best in the 1,500 meters and second place in the 400 meters. Making All-America in 1982-83, DiCarlo also won the NCAA Championship at 500 yards, a U.S.Open record.

At the summer Olympics of 1984 he won the 400-meter freestyle, becoming the first UA athlete to earn an individual gold medal. (At the U.S. trials he also won the 400- as well as the 1,600-meter freestyles.)

"It's funny to think about the Olympics now," he says. "It's easy to forget the pain, the hard work and all the days I threw my goggles in the gutter and said, 'Forget it, this hurts too much.'"

Rather than rest on his laurels, DiCarlo returned to Arizona to swim out his last year. At the 1985 NCAA Championships, he finished second in the 500-yard freestyle, again earning All-America honors.

Following graduation, he became an industrial real estate broker in his hometown, Denver. In 1990 he was inducted into the UA Sports Hall of Fame.

another future Olympian, Ed Mendoza, became the school's first NCAA cross country All-American, placing 15th, followed by a ninth place finish the following year.

Arizona's cross country star of the late 1970s was Thom Hunt, who earned an unprecedented four straight All-America awards, placing in the top 10 at the NCAA meet three times, and leading the Wildcats to top 10 national finishes in 1976, 1977 and 1978.

By then Arizona was well on its way to becoming one of the nation's premier men's collegiate cross country programs. Murray's harriers captured their first Pac-10 team title in 1983, and from then, through 1991, the Wildcats won five team and three individual conference championships, finished in the top 10 in the NCAA meet five times, and narrowly missed a national title with a second-place finish behind Arkansas in 1984.

The University hosted the NCAA men's and women's championships in 1986, placing sixth, as Wildcat Aaron Ramirez won the individual title, and again in 1991, when the men's team tied for fourth. In addition to Ramirez's Pac-10 and NCAA titles, two UA runners, Tom Ansberry, 1982-83, and Marc Davis, 1989-90, have won back-to back Pac-10 crowns. All told, 13 different runners have earned All-America honors 22 times.

Cross country became a women's varsity sport in 1976 and men's coach Dave Murray also headed up the women's program from 1977 to 1981. New women's track coach Chris Murray (no relation to Dave) took over the women harriers in 1982 and served through 1989, when both programs were put back under Dave Murray.

Led by three-time All-American and 1984 U.S. Olympian Joan Hansen, Arizona won three straight team titles in the Western Collegiate Athletic Conference (WCAA), 1979-81, placed fifth in the AIAW meet in 1979 and second in 1980, and eighth in the first NCAA Women's Championship in 1981, but did not qualify as a team the next nine years. In 1988 Bridget Smyth became the UA's first female cross country All-American in seven years, placing 20th. In

During the sport's rocky, abbreviated tenure at Arizona, men's gymnastics was not without outstanding performers. The most distinguished was Pat Arnold (1966-68), two-time Western Athletic Conference champion on the still rings and in 1968, national champion and first team All-America. *Courtesy, University of Arizona Athletic Department.*

1991, under the guidance of new assistant coach Sue Parks, the Wildcat women recorded their highest Pac-10 finish ever (2nd) and placed 11th at the NCAA meet in Tucson.

Women's Gymnastics

Women's gymnastics began intercollegiate competition in 1971-72, winning two regional titles and an AIAW 11th place in 1973, but made little else on the regional or national level for the next 10 years. Since taking over as head coach in 1980, Jim Gault has developed the team into one of the nation's finest, making its first NCAA appearance in 1984.

Stacy Fowlkes transferred to Arizona from Cal State-Fullerton in 1991, just in time to help lead the UA Gymcats to fifth place at the NCAA Championships, their highest finish ever. In the process she earned All-American honors with fifth place finishes on the uneven bars and, tying with teammate Jenna Karodbil, on the balance beam. *Photo: Robert F. Walker. University Photo Center.*

The following year Mary Kay Brown and Kelly Chaplin became the first Wildcats to earn All-America honors.

Since 1987 the UA has qualified for the NCAA Championships every year, capped by an all-time high finish of fifth in 1992. The Gymcats have also been one of the most competitive UA teams since Pac-10 women's competition began in 1987, finishing second behind UCLA in 1988 and 1990, just missing their first league title by .15 points to Oregon State at the 1992 conference meet held in McKale Center. Anna Basaldua, who won the school's first NCAA women's gymnastics title in the vault in 1991, also scored the UA's first ever perfect 10 in the vault at the 1992 Pac-10 meet.

Gault has been recognized with league Coach of the Year honors in 1984, 1985, 1986 and 1989. He also coached the U.S. team at the

World University Games in Yugoslavia in 1987.

Men's and Women's Swimming and Diving

Swimming began at Arizona in 1928, and looked like it might have a future when the fledgling Wildcat tankers recorded a stunning upset of USC, 32-27. However, financial difficulties dunked the sport after just two more seasons. It resurfaced on the varsity level in 1946.

Charles Ott served as head coach for 22 of the next 25 years, but limited financial support for recruiting and scholarships kept the program well below any national prominence for a quarter of a century. Arizona did win four official and several other unofficial Border Conference titles in the post-war era.

When Arizona entered the Western Athletic Conference in 1962, the program was still hampered by inferior facilities. The Wildcats were perennial league doormats, finishing last in eight of the WAC's first 10 championships while winning only one individual title.

The completion of the long-awaited and much needed Olympic-sized pool in 1974 was the impetus that finally had swimming upgraded to the level of other UA sports. Olympian Charles Hickcox was hired in 1972 to begin rebuilding the program, taking the Wildcats from eighth to fourth in the WAC in 1973 and a winning attitude as well. UA grad Bob Davis succeeded Hickcox in 1974, and quickly built the program into a national power while winning four straight WAC championships, 1975-78.

Under Davis, Arizona scored its first ever points in the NCAA Championships in 1976, placed 11th in 1977 and 1978, and had 13 swimmers earn 22 All-America recognition. Standouts on Davis's teams included Olympians Rick DeMont and Doug Northway, who transferred to the UA after Washington de-emphasized the sport. Davis left following the 1978 seasons to become an associate athletic director and executive director of the UA Wildcat Club.

Chosen to take Arizona into the Pac-10 era was Dick Jochums, the head coach at Long Beach State who had an extensive background as a U.S. national team coach and developer of world-class swimmers such as 1975 Sullivan Award winner Tim Shaw, who would transfer to and swim for the UA.

Jochums would lead the UA men to top 12 or better NCAA finishes in eight of his 10 seasons as head coach and develop some of the UA most prominent pool performers, including UA's first NCAA champion, Doug Towne, who won the 500-yard freestyle in 1981; 1984 Olympic gold and silver medalist George DiCarlo; Australian Olympic

GREAT MOMENTS

WILDCATS ON THE PGA AND LPGA TOUR

At left, CHRIS JOHNSON

It takes dedication, tenacity, and attention to details to make it on the LPGA and PGA Tour. These UA golfers have shown they have the stuff that pros are made of. The same hard work, perseverance, and emphasis on components has made Weiser Lock the nation's second largest maker of residential door locks. From its humble beginnings in California as a foundry in 1904, Weiser Lock's Tucson plant now occupies more than 240,000 square feet of production capability. Weiser utilizes the most modern equipment and manufacturing techniques available within the industry in the fabrication of its WeiserBolt Series of Locks.

MARK STUDLEY
President, Weiser Lock

The UA golf program has produced some perennial winners. These former Wildcat golfers had tour cards for 1991 PGA and LPGA play:

Chris Johnson: 1990 LPGA season with five career victories and $993,798 in official money winnings. As of 1991, she is 23rd on the LPGA's career money list.

Johnson joined the tour in July 1980, only a few months following her graduation from the UA where she was All-American in 1979 and 1980 and won the individual championship of the Western Collegiate Athletic Association in 1980.

Professionally she has won the 1984 Samaritan Turquoise Classic (Phoenix), 1984 Tucson Conquistadors Open, 1986 GNA/Glendale Federal Classic, 1987 Columbia Savings LPGA National Pro-Am and the 1990 Atlantic City Classic.

Robert Gamez's first season was spectacular; he won the Northern Telecom Tucson Open and the Nestle Invitational and was named Rookie of the Year with $461,407 for 27th on the money list.

ROBERT GAMEZ

Dan Pohl returned to competition in 1991 after missing the entire 1990 tour due to a back operation. Fortunately, he won the 1986 NEC World Series of Golf, earning a 10-year exemption. Pohl entered 1991 with $2,328,363 career money winnings. In 1986 he won the 1986 Colonial and the World Series. It was his best tour year with $463,630 for fifth place on the money list. He won the1987 Vardon Trophy (awarded for the lowest stroke average on the PGA Tour) and was on the U.S. Ryder Cup team. Pohl represents The Boulders Resort in Carefree, Arizona.

DAN POHL

Don Pooley entered the 1991 season with $2,181,005 in career winnings. He won the 1980 B.C. Open, the 1987 Memorial Tournament, was co-winner of the 1983 Jerry Ford Invitational and won the 1989 Ebel Match Play title. Pooley won the 1985 Vardon Trophy and ranked 83rd on the 1990-money list with $192,570, including a third place in the Memorial.

DON POOLEY

He turned pro after his 1973 graduation from Arizona. His best year on the tour was 1980, with $450,005 in winnings for 18th on the money list. He won the million dollar hole-in-one in the 1987 Bay Hill Classic. Pooley represents the La Paloma Resort of Tucson.

Larry Silveira earned his PGA Card in qualifying school in 1988, 1989 and 1990. He completed his Wildcat eligibility in 1988 and turned professional that year. Silveira entered the 1990 season with $126,407 in career winnings. He was 158th on the money list in 1989.

LARRY SILVEIRA

Mike Springer earned his PGA Tour Card by finishing fourth on the 1990 Hogan Tour money list with $82,906. He won the inaugural Hogan Tour event, the 1990 Bakersfield Open and came from behind on the last day to win the El Paso Open. He completed his collegiate eligibility in 1988 and turned professional that same year.

MIKE SPRINGER

medalist Peter Evans; two-time World University Games 1,500-meter free champ Alex Mlawsky and national champion backstroker Scott Johnson. Arizona's other NCAA champion during the '80s was Polish Olympian Mariusz Podkoscielny; who won the 1,650-yard freestyle, and set four school records as a freshman in the 1989 NCAA meet, coached by interim head coach Chuck Knoles.

Under a storm of controversy, over an ineligible swimmer and other irregularities in the program, Jochums resigned in December 1988. He was replaced on an interim basis by Chuck Knoles, who finished out the 1989 season. In 1990 Frank Busch was named to run the program and quickly established himself as one of the nation's top young coaches.

In 1991 he was named Pac-10 Women's Coach of the Year and his first two seasons produced eight men's school records and 13 All-Americans while leading the men's team to a 10th place NCAA finish in 1990 and a highest-ever seventh in 1991.

One of the first women's sports at the University to achieve national success was swimming. The program began in 1973, and in 1975, led by 1972 U.S. Olympian Dana Shrader and diver Laurie Brunet, the Wildcats placed fifth in the AIAW Championships held at Tempe. In 1978 Diane Johnson became the first UA woman to win a national collegiate title, winning the 400-yard individual medley at the AIAW meet.

Top-10 AIAW finishes were also recorded in 1980 (7th) and 1981 (9th), as Johnson won her second collegiate title, this time in the 200-meter. At the first NCAA Women's Swimming Championships in 1982, Johnson won the 50-yard freestyle and earned All-America honors in five individual events and two relays, scoring 75 of UA's 179 points to place her team in sixth place.

Other UA aquatic stars of the AIAW and early NCAA period were Beth Lutz, who earned All-America honors in 12 individual and relay events between 1978-81 and set six world records for the deaf. Diver Michele Mitchell, a four-year collegiate All-American, would go on to become the top U.S. women's diver of the 1980s, winning platform silver medals at the 1984 and 1988 Olympics in addition to numerous other national and international cham-

QUOTABLES

"I have always been very impressed with the spirit and patronage there is in Tucson for the UA athletic program. My wife and I attended school on the East Coast but we are now true fans of the Cats. The enthusiasm and support we see for University of Arizona sports says a lot for the people of the community and makes Tucson the great place it is to live."

CHRISTOPHER J. TSIGHIS
Senior VP & District Manager,
Grubb & Ellis Company

Arizona's Aaron Ramirez (#811) leads the field midway through the 1986 NCAA men's cross-country championship, held at Tucson's Canada Hills Country Club. Ramirez went on to victory, becoming Arizona's first national champion in cross-country, and teammate Matt Giusto (just behind Ramirez) finished third. *Courtesy, University of Arizona Athletic Department.*

pionships and honors.

Jochums also coached the UA women for six years, taking over in 1983. Some of his standouts were All-American and national 1987 U.S. long-course 200-meter freestyle champion Francie O'Leary, and 1988 Pac-10 Co-Swimmer of the Year Cheryl Simmons, who was NCAA runner-up in both the 500- and 1,650-yard freestyles in 1988.

Busch guided the UA men's and women's teams to their highest combined finish ever at the 1990 NCAA meets; the men placed 10th with their second-highest-ever point total, 154, and the women, which just four entries, finished a creditable 14th with 76 points. The following year both teams placed seventh, the men scoring a record point total of 195, and future Olympic triple medalist Crissy Ahmann-Leighton, setting an American record of 52.36 in the 100-yard butterfly.

The year 1992 would be the crowning achievement in the history of University of Arizona swimming. Both men's and women's teams recorded their highest NCAA finish ever, placing fifth. Only a relay disqualification kept the women from placing third.

The Wildcat women were led once again by Ahmann-Leighton, who lowered her American record in the 100-yard butterfly to 51.75 and set school records with a second and third, respectively, in the the 50- and 100-yard freestyles, and paced the UA to runner-up finishes in two relays. Arizona's total of 272 points was nearly 100 more than its previous women's best

The 1990 NCAA champion on the vault, Anna Basaldua battled through debilitating injuries in 1991, was named All Pac-10 and helped lead Arizona to a fifth place finish at the NCAA Women's Gymnastics Championships, its highest finish ever. Shown with her is her appreciative coach, Jim Gault. *Photo: Robert F. Walker. University Photo Center.*

of 179 in 1982.

The UA men, led by junior sprinter and butterflyer Seth Pepper and distance freestyle ace Podkoscielny, scored 238 points, topping the previous year's total of 195. Pepper was runner-up in the 100-yard butterfly for the second straight year and was a finalist in both the 50- and 100-yard frees, setting school records in all three events. Podkoscielny finished second in the 500 free for the fourth straight year and also recorded his fourth top three 1,650 free finish.

NOTABLES

Here's an early photo of how aspiring UA polo players of the 1930s learned proper technique. In some years, there were more students trying out for the polo team than for the football squad.

Courtesy, Arizona Alumni Association.

MEN'S AND WOMEN'S GOLF

Golf got its start at the University of Arizona in 1935 under legendary basketball coach Fred A. Enke, who served as head coach for 32 years until his retirement following the 1966 season. Arizona dominated the sport in the old Border Conference, winning 23 titles between 1936 and 1961, competing in its first NCAA Tournament in 1941.

In 1960 and 1961 Arizona golf teams, led by top players such as honorable mention All-Americans Mike Rombold, Tom Finke and Payne Palmer, placed seventh in consecutive NCAA Championship tournaments. Top UA links performer during the Western Athletic Conference era (1963-78) was the school's first All-American, Drue Johnson. He was conference medalist in 1969 and tied for second in the NCAA tournament in 1967 and 1969.

In 1971 Arizona hosted the NCAA Championship at the Tucson National Golf Club. Wildcat golf stars of the 1970s included future PGA standouts Dan Pohl, who placed fifth in the 1977 NCAA meet, and Don Pooley.

Enke's successor as head coach had been former UA football assistant Roy Tatum. He served for five years and was succeeded in 1973 by John Gibson, who was followed in 1979 by Rick LaRose who switched from coaching a nationally ranked water polo program (the sport was discontinued in 1979) to head coach of a men's golf program that had qualified for the NCAAs just once in the previous 16 years.

Hard work and perseverance have paid off for LaRose, who has established Arizona men's golf as one of the nation's elite collegiate programs, winning the NCAA title in 1992.

His first team in 1979 placed second in the

first Pac-10 tournament. However, it took almost the rest of the decade for the program to reach the level it has attained in the last five seasons. Paul Nolen was the UA's first conference medalist in 1984, and the team breakthrough came in 1987 when the Wildcats won their first Pac-10 title led by medalist Larry Silveira. That was followed by three straight second-place finishes and another title in 1991. Pac-10 Golfer of the Year honors were won by Larry Silveira in 1988 Robert Gamez in 1989, and Manny Zerman was the 1991 conference medalist.

During water polo's brief, six-year visit to the UA campus, coach Rick LaRose led the Wildcats to a record of 118-49-3, three NCAA District 7 championships, and four NCAA top ten finishes. The sport became an economic casualty after the 1979 season, and LaRose began another successful career as the UA men's golf coach. *Courtesy, University of Arizona Athletic Department.*

The 1987 team was second-ranked nationally going into the NCAA tourney but placed only 18th. The 1988 team garnered the school's first ever number one ranking during the season, finished sixth at the NCAA and Eric Meeks won the U.S. Amateur title. Arizona was sixth in the NCAA again in 1989, finishing second in the Pac-10 and NCAA. Both he and Meeks were members of the U.S. Walker Cup team.

NOTABLES

Long after his retirement, Fred Enke remained extremely popular with many of his former UA players, both basketball and golfers, as this clever invitation to his 83rd birthday celebration attests.

Photo by: University Photo Center. Courtesy, University of Arizona Athletic Department.

Arizona got the new decade off in style with the school's highest NCAA golf finish ever, third at the 1990 Championship. The following year, after winning the Pac-10 and NCAA West Regional, the Wildcats bombed out on the tough Poppy Hill course at Pebble Beach, California, and ended up a frustrated 18th.

Redemption for the disaster of the year before would come in 1992, as Arizona finally achieved the highest level of collegiate golf—an NCAA championship. The Wildcats beat archrival Arizona State by seven strokes, finishing with an NCAA tournament record 23-under par team total of 1,129 on the University of New Mexico's South Course. Arizona was led by senior Harry Rudolph, who

Junior Manny Zerman was a season-long standout for coach Rick LaRose as the Wildcat men's golf team won its first NCAA championship in 1992. Zerman and teammates Harry Rudolph and David Berganio earned All-America honors. *Courtesy, University of Arizona Athletic Department.*

placed second and earned first-team All-America honors, and Zerman, who placed third.

LaRose, who was named NCAA Coach of the Year, said: "Our goal was to shoot under par for every round, and we did. This is something I've been dreaming about for 14 years. There was a lot of pressure on us going in because we were ranked No. 1. But our guys stood up to it and came through when it counted.

"Believe me, there is nothing like winning a national championship!"

Although it is yet to win a national title, women's golf has also flourished at the UA since its inception as a collegiate sport in 1972. That year the Wildcats posted a second place finish in the first AIAW National Championship, and under coaches Sandy Eggert, JoAnne Weinheimer and Joanne Lusk would record seven top 10 national finishes over the next eight seasons, including fourth in 1973 and 1979. Arizona women's golf, featuring LPGA standouts Susie Berdoy and Chris Johnson, who was an All-American in 1979 and 1980 and won the WCAA individual title in 1980, was ranked in the top 20 nationally from 1972 through 1983. In 1975 the university hosted the AIAW Championship Tournament at Tucson's Oro Valley Country Club.

In 1984 Lusk was succeeded by Kim Haddow, who has guided UA women's golf into the ranks of the national elite. From 1988 through 1992 the Wildcats have been ranked first or second nationally, achieving consecutive NCAA placing of twelfth, eighth, fourth, seventh, third and second.

Although Fred A. Enke is known principally as one of America's finest college basketball coaches, he was also responsible for the creation and evolution of the UA men's golf program. Enke guided the Wildcat golfers for 31 years (1935-1966) to nine Border Conference championships and two seventh place NCAA finishes. *Courtesy, University of Arizona Athletic Department.*

Back-to-back NCAA individual titles were won in 1990 and 1991 by Susan Slaughter, who had been runner-up as a freshman in 1989, and Annika Sorenstam in 1991. After runner-up finishes to UCLA in 1990 and 1991, the UA won its first Pac-10 women's golf title in 1992 by a record 33 strokes over Arizona State, as three Wildcat players finished in the top four. Sorenstam won the individual title, sophomore Leta Lindley tied for second and Ulrika Johansson was third.

Arizona entered the 1992 NCAA Championship at Arizona State ranked number one and as the strong favorite to win its first NCAA title. However, after a terrible first day in which they fell nine strokes off the pace, the Wildcats had to settle for second by four strokes, 1,175-1,171, behind second-ranked San Jose State. San Jose State was the only team to beat the UA all season.

Sorenstam, seeking to become the first repeat winner in NCAA history, placed second by three strokes with a five-under par 283, seven strokes better than her winning total the previous year.

"We really wanted to win and we had the opportunity," said Haddow, of the disappointing second place finish. She was named Pac-10 Coach of the Year and National and Regional Coach of the Year by the National Golf Coaches Association. "We played well and we're proud to be second. We just didn't capitalize when we had the opportunity. I'm just sad the season's over."

Men's and Women's Tennis

Tennis has had a long history at the university, with students playing matches with the Tucson Tennis Club as early as 1901. Despite rough dirt courts and inadequate equipment, both men and women players participated in local and state tournaments and occasional matches with local and state high schools, private schools and club teams.

The first match that could actually be considered intercollegiate competition took place on December 12, 1913, when UA players won singles and doubles from Tempe Normal. Varsity letters were first awarded in 1913, and in 1921 matches were played against Occidental, Redlands, USC and Pomona College.

The sport got its first real boost in 1924 when four concrete courts were built near the Steward Observatory building. Then C. Zaner "Zip" Lesher, who was instrumental in founding the Border Conference in 1931, volunteered to serve as the school's first permanent tennis coach in 1932. The first conference tournament was held in 1933, Arizona winning both the singles and doubles titles, and the Wildcats dominated the sport during the league's existence (1932-61), winning 21 team titles, 21 "A" singles and 15 "A" doubles championships.

In 1947 Tom Van Fleet and Herb Benham were the first Arizona players to compete in the

NCAA Championships, as did one of the top UA players of the 1950s, Jimmy Dye, who reached the second round in 1953. Lesher retired in 1959 and was replaced by Dave Snyder, a former SWC doubles champion at Texas and a nationally ranked player. In his 12 seasons at Arizona, Snyder developed a number of prominent players, including three-time All-Americans Bill Lenoir (1962-64) and Brian Cheney (1967-69), won three Western Athletic Conference titles and posted consecutive NCAA top 10 finishes from 1963 through 1970, the highest being third in 1967.

Under Snyder and Bill Murphy, who succeeded him in 1973, Arizona won six WAC titles, more than any other conference school. Murphy, a former Michigan coach who had won 11 Big Ten titles and an NCAA crown in 1957, posted a 98-47 record in dual matches and won three WAC titles, and and his 1974 team placed eighth in the NCAA tournament.

Fittingly, the accomplishments of the two best tennis players in UA history—Bill Lenoir (above) and Brian Cheney (below)—are almost identical. Both Lenoir (1962-64) and Cheney (1967-69) were two-time WAC Champions, twice NCAA singles quarter finalists, and three-time All Americans. Lenoir was also a WAC scholar-athlete award winner and Cheney, also NCAA runner-up in doubles, led Arizona to a third place NCAA finish in 1967, its highest ever. *Courtesy, University of Arizona Athletic Department.*

A new and daunting era for Arizona tennis dawned in 1979 when the Wildcats joined the Pacific-10 Conference, far and away the strongest grouping of national powers in collegiate tennis. Battling the talent-loaded California schools of the Pac-10, especially for the men's team, has been a frustrating and mostly losing proposition for Arizona, although the women have been able to make some notable headway.

Through 1991, all 10 NCAA women's titles contested have been won by either Stanford or Southern Cal. And since the team dual-match tournament format was adopted in 1977, Pac-10 South schools Stanford, UCLA or USC have won 14 of 16 NCAA crowns.

Under Ted Kissell, who replaced Murphy in 1981 and served until 1986, and current coach Bill Wright, the UA men have have held their own outside of the league. However in 14 years of league play, the Cats are only 23-111 against Pac-10 Southern Division teams, all but seven of those victories coming against Arizona State. In Six-Pac men's tennis, Arizona has beaten Stanford and USC once a piece, California five times, and has never won a road dual match on one of the four California schools' home courts.

Kissell was Pac-10 Coach of the Year in 1981 when the Wildcats earned their highest final-season ranking, tied for 16th, and in 1982 his team posted its best Six-Pac dual meet record ever, 4-6. However, the Arizona men have yet to qualify as a team for the NCAA tournament since the single-elimination dual match play format was adopted in 1977. Paul Chamberlin in 1984 and Doug Livingston in 1991 are the only UA men's players to earn All-America honors during the Pac-10 era.

Senior Banni Redhair teamed with Danielle Scott to make up one of the finest doubles combinations in the country. Coach Becky Bell's Wildcats beat both USC and UCLA on the road for the first time ever and captured the Pac-10 singles, doubles and team titles. Redhair, Scott and Alix Creek were named All-America; Redhair was named Academic All America as well. *Photo: Robert F. Walker. University Photo Center.*

Tennis was one of the few sports at the University of Arizona that provided high-level competitive opportunities for women before the institution of varsity-level intercollegiate competition in the 1970s. UA women began competing locally and in statewide and regional events along with the men shortly after the turn of the century and continued to do so. Some of the top UA women's athletes of the '40s and '50s, such as Marie Jacks, Maxine McCain and Mari Bailey, were outstanding tennis players who won many local, state and regional titles.

The Arizona Intercollegiate, established in in 1947 is one of the longest standing women's college tennis events in the nation, and throughout the '50s and '60s UA women were playing dual matches with Arizona State and other area schools in addition to competing in a variety of team and individual tournaments.

Official varsity competition began in 1972, but it was not until Ann Lebedeff was named head coach in 1978 that UA women's tennis achieved a national ranking. In 1981 the Wildcats were ranked 15th nationally after reaching the consolation semi-finals of the AIAW Championship at Tempe, and in 1982 Arizona qualified for the first NCAA Women's Championships, losing to eventual runner-up UCLA, 9-0, in the first round. In 1985, Lebedeff's final UA team was ranked as high as 9th nationally, but lost to California, 6-3, in the first round of the NCAA tourney.

Lebedeff left in 1985 to pursue a doctorate in sports administration, and was succeeded by Becky Bell, a former All-America player at and assistant for the top-rated UCLA program. Under Bell, the UA women have qualified for the NCAA team championship tournament every year since 1988, advancing to the second round in 1989 and 1990 with victories over Texas A&M 5-1 and BYU.

Probably the top individual performance of the '80s came in February 1988 when the doubles team of Betsy Somerville-Sue Russo was ranked number one after winning the Rolex-ITCA National Indoor Collegiate Championships in Minneapolis. In 1991, the UA women posted their best Pac-10 South record ever, 5-5, and Danielle Scott earned All-America honors.

It was a banner year for Arizona women's tennis in 1992 as UA players won both singles and doubles titles at the April 23-26 Pac-10 Individual Championships, in Ojai, California. Sophomore Alix Creek claimed the singles crown and then paired with Scott to win doubles. Three UA players, Scott, Creek and Banni Redhair earned All-America honors, and Redhair was an Academic All-American. As a team, the Wildcats were ranked ninth in the final ITCA/Volvo (Intercollegiate Tennis Coaches Association) rankings, but lost to Arizona State, 5-4, in their first round NCAA match.

University of Arizona Individual Sports Statistical Highlights

Intercollegiate Track and Field Champions

NCAA	Name	Event
1992	Tanya Hughes	High Jump
1991	Tanya Hughes	High Jump
1989	Derek Huff	Decathlon
1989	Marc Davis	5,000-Meter Run
1989	Carla Garrett	Shotput (I)
1989	Carla Garrett	Shotput
1989	Carla Garrett	Discus
1988	Matt Giusto	5,000-Meter Run
1986	Katrena Johnson	High-Jump
1985	Katrena Johnson	High-Jump
1984	Ruth Waithera-Nganga	400-Meter Run (I)
1983	Meg Ritchie	Shotput
1982	Vance Johnson	Long-Jump
1982	Meg Ritchie	Shotput
1982	Meg Ritchie	Discus
1965	Gayle Hopkins	Long-Jump
1965	John Tushaus	Javelin

AIAW	Name	Event
1982	Charmaine Gale	High-Jump
1981	Robin Marks	400-Meter Hurdles
1981	Meg Ritchie	Shotput (I)
1981	Meg Ritchie	Shotput
1980	Meg Ritchie	Shotput
1980	Meg Ritchie	Discus

Men's Cross Country

Years	Coach
1968- Present	Dave Murray *Four Conference Championships* *Highest NCAA Finish - 2nd, in 1984*
1958-1967	Carl Cooper *One Conference Championship, 1962*

Women's Cross Country

Years	Coach
1990-Present	Dave Murray
1982-89	Chris Murray
1978-81	Dave Murray *Three Conference Championships* *Highest NCAA Finish- 2nd, in 1980*
1977	Phil Stanforth
1976	Peggy Anderson

Men's Swimming and Diving NCAA Champions

Year	Name	Event
1989	Mariusz Podkoscielny	1,650 Freestyle
1984	George Di Carlo	500 Freestyle
1983	George Di Carlo	500 Freestyle
1981	Doug Towne	500 Freestyle

Women's Swimming and Diving NCAA Champions

Year	Name	Event
1992	Crissy Ahmann-Leighton	100 Butterfly
1991	Crissy Ahmann-Leighton	100 Butterfly
1982	Diane Johnson	50 Freestyle

Women's Golf

Year	Coach	Conference	NCAA
1992	Kim Haddow	1st	2nd
1991	Kim Haddow	2nd	3rd
1990	Kim Haddow	2nd	7th
1989	Kim Haddow	3rd	4th
1988	Kim Haddow	5th	8th
1987	Kim Haddow	4th	12th

Men's Golf

Year	Coach	Conference	NCAA
1992	Rick LaRose	4th	1st
1991	Rick LaRose	1st	1st
1990	Rick LaRose	2nd	4th
1989	Rick LaRose	2nd	1st
1988	Rick LaRose	2nd	
1987	Rick LaRose	1st	

Women's Gymnastics All-Time Records

Year	Record-Holder	Event
1992	Anna Basaldua	Vault
1992	Stacy Fowlkes	Uneven Parallel Bars
1991	Diana Rendall	Uneven Parallel Bars
1992	Stacy Fowlkes	Balance Beam
1992	Jenna Karadbil (2 times)	Balance Beam
1992	Stacy Fowlkes	Floor Exercise
1992	Kristi Gunning	Floor Exercise
1991	Anna Basaldua (4 times)	Floor Exercise
1989	Diane Monty	Floor Exercise
1989	Noelle Schnurpfeil	Floor Exercise
1992	Stacy Fowlkes	All-Around

As the Wildcats strive to maintain and increase their successful effort to become one of the top-rated intercollegiate athletic programs in the United States, support from UA alumni and friends has become more crucial than ever.

The University of Arizona's athletic teams have always had a continued commitment to greatness. In recent years Wildcat athletic teams have played in three football bowl games, won four conference basketball championships, won both the conference title and the College World Series championship in baseball and softball, and participated in numerous

PARTNERS IN EXCELLENCE

UA fans pack Arizona Stadium to cheer on the Wildcats. *Photo: Chris Mooney/Baflour Walker.*

postseason events in other sports. Former Wildcat stars now play in the American and National baseball leagues, the National Football League, and the National Basketball Association.

Frank Sancet Baseball Field. *Courtesy, University of Arizona Athletic Department.*

Many UA athletes have been successful Olympic contenders and have brought home medals for their country.

The Wildcats' male athletes compete in eight sports; women take part in nine. Wildcat supporters can take pride in the total athletic program available at the UA.

Not surprisingly, the UA athletic department has an ongoing need to upgrade and remodel its facilities—and sometimes to build new ones. The UA cannot use legislative-appropriated monies for these vital capital improvements, and gifts from alumni and friends have been indispensable in funding athletic facilities.

Many of the important additions to the UA athletic complex have been made possible all or in part by such gifts. These include the Fred A. Enke Plaza, new dugouts and batting cage at Sancet Field, remodeling of the football and men's basketball locker rooms, remodeling of the Women's Intercollegiate Locker Room, the Hillenbrand Aquatic Center, the La Nelle Robson Tennis Center, the Roy P. Drachman Track & Field Complex, the Timm T. Hackley Strength Training Center, the Waldo Dicus Student-Athlete Services Center, and the John "Button" Salmon Memorial.

McKale Memorial Center. *Courtesy, Arizona Alumni Association.*

The Arizona athletic program, the Tucson community, UA active alumni, Wildcat fans and friends are all bound by a common purpose—to enable student athletes to accomplish achievements that will direct the national athletic spotlight on the University of Arizona.

Hillenbrand Aquatic Center. *Photo: Susan Hamilton. Courtesy, University of Arizona Athletic Department.*

The UA athletic department is really an extension of the involvement of others. Together they have formed the most enviable team in Arizona—alumni, friends, the administrators, coaches, and student athletes. These partners in excellence can get the job done only with the help of everyone on the team.

Wildcat fever on a Sa[illegible] afternoon. *Photo: Edward McCain.*

Cats
Cats

THE UNIVERSITY OF ARIZONA DEPARTMENT OF INTERCOLLEGIATE ATHLETICS

The University of Arizona's first organized athletic competition was a "Field Day" held on February 22, 1897, at Tucson's Union Park racetrack. Following band music, speeches, and other festivities, 19 young men from the university and the town competed in eight track-and-field events. One of the day's highlights was a pole vault of 8'10" by Frank Groesbeck, a first-year preparatory student. The price of admission was 25 cents, and the gate receipts were to be used for the erection of a new flagpole in front of the university's main building, which was separated from the town of Tucson itself by miles of undeveloped desert. (That building would not officially be designated "Old Main" until 1927.)

Two years passed before the formation of the university's first official athletic team, the 1899 football squad. The 16 players on its roster played three games and finished with a win, a loss and a tie. They were not called "wildcats" or any other name, just "the university team."

The city limits of Tucson now extend many miles in all directions beyond the University of Arizona campus, and the current UA athletic program seems light years removed from the meager sports endeavors of the late 1890s. Today's UA Wildcats compete in 17 NCAA Division I sports (nine women's, eight men's) and in the Pacific 10 Conference, arguably the most prominent and competitive academic/athletic conference in the nation. Conference, regional and national honors for UA teams and individual student-athletes are now commonplace, and the overall athletic program has become one of the most recognized and accomplished in America.

The university's extremely popular "desert" or "cactus" logo is unique in intercollegiate sports. The logo is the sole property of the UA athletic department.

A complex combination of education, athletic competition, public entertainment, entrepreneurship, and charitable enterprise, the UA Department of Intercollegiate Athletics is also a valuable partner in the local economy. With a full- and part-time staff of about 200 people, the UA Athletic Department would easily qualify as one of southern Arizona's top 200 employers.

An independent survey in 1989 conservatively concluded that the economic impact of each UA home football game is approximately $370,000. Over a six-game home football schedule, the total economic benefit to Tucson is more than $2.2 million a year. This figure is for only one sport. It would increase substantially if the impact of the UA men's basketball schedule—about 18 sold-out home games yearly—and its other at-home competitions and special events were included.

The University of Arizona's unique, popular desert logo is the exclusive property of the U of A Athletic Department.

ERROL L. MONTGOMERY & ASSOCIATES, INC.

Errol L. Montgomery & Associates, Inc., or simply M&A, is a groundwater consulting group that provides professional hydrogeologic services in nearly all aspects of the search for groundwater supplies, construction and development of high-capacity water wells, and control and management of this valuable resource. The consulting firm works chiefly for mining and manufacturing concerns across the United States and in South America.

LEFT Errol Montgomery (second from left) reviews the results of a hydrogeologic investigation with professional staff members of Errol L. Montgomery & Associates, Inc.

Many of the activities of the company today are related to groundwater contamination. This work involves construction of groundwater monitor wells, analysis of groundwater flow and contaminant transport, construction of computer-based groundwater models to predict the effectiveness of various clean-up alternatives, and implementation of remedial actions.

Although M&A is often involved in well-publicized projects, many of the firm's efforts are unheralded.

"Most of our work is confidential. For example, our work in exploration for new groundwater sources here and in South America is particularly sensitive. Inadvertent release of information on location and magnitude of projects could badly damage our clients' competitive position in a very competitive industry," explains Dr. Errol L. Montgomery, president of M&A.

At its Tucson office M&A maintains a permanent staff of 36 people, including 25 professionals and 11 support personnel. The professional staff comprises hydrogeologists, hydrologists, geological engineers, soil physicists, hydrochemists, and computer specialists, all with national and/or international experience. Nearly all of the professional staff have advanced degrees, many from the internationally recognized Department of Hydrology at the University of Arizona.

Among the multitude of professional hydrogeologic services available from M&A are the evaluation of hydrogeologic conditions, preparation of plans for groundwater control systems, design and supervision of groundwater exploration and development programs, evaluation of groundwater adequacy for compliance with state regulatory agencies, formulation and implementation of remedial actions to correct groundwater contamination, preparation of technical reports, and investigations for expert trial testimony.

"This firm does nearly all types of work related to groundwater," says Montgomery.

The Tucson office of Errol L. Montgomery & Associates, Inc. sprawls throughout 10,000 square feet of garden office space. One of the unusual and highly valuable features of the Tucson office is a comprehensive technical library.

"In some aspects of our field, we have a better selection of research materials and books than the University of Arizona," says Montgomery.

BELOW A drilling rig constructs a groundwater monitor well south of Tucson. Monitor wells are used to monitor water level and water quality.

THE MILES LABEL COMPANY, INC.

The Miles Label Company, Inc., is both a successful entrepreneurial enterprise and a family affair.

Russell Hubert Miles started the printing company in his garage in Des Moines, Iowa, during the summer of 1912. Five generations of family members have worked for the company since then.

The Miles Label Company manufactures millions of labels and business forms annually.

Paul Wilson Miles, Russell's son, began wintering in Tucson in 1948. He moved the company to Tucson permanently in June 1962. His son, Robert H. Miles, recently retired following 44 years at the helm of The Miles Label Company

Today Robert's son, Paul W. Miles, is president of the company. He began working as a letterpressman for the company while still a student at Tucson's Catalina High School. Paul's son, P. J. Miles, currently acts as corporate secretary/treasurer.

Jim Lupori, vice president and part owner of The Miles Label Company, joined with the Miles family in July 1977. He is a graduate of the University of Arizona.

The Miles Label Company manufactures millions of labels and business forms annually. About 80 percent of its business is produced for Tucson-based enterprises, and the remaining 20 percent is shipped to national companies.

The Miles Label Company has a full-time artist on staff and also produces all of its own printing plates.

"Each label or form goes through a variety of processes that are all very specialized and mechanical," explains Miles.

The company has a six-color press, two three-color presses, and a two-color press. Support equipment includes a typesetting computer, an eight-station collator, a computerized camera, an envelope press, and folder and bindery equipment.

The Miles Label Company has machinery that can simultaneously print the front and back of a label or form, reverse print for inside window application, roll or fanfold, laminate, and die cut.

Snap-out and computer business forms that follow true accounting lines are a frequently requested item at The Miles Label Company. Through the use of these innovative multiple part forms and computer forms (standard design or custom design), a company can generate a customer invoice or receipt, take inventory, and do a cost accounting at the same time.

"Computers have totally revolutionized the commercial printing business. But no matter how technologically advanced The Miles Label Company becomes, or how large we grow, our mission will remain the same—to serve our clients and meet their specialized needs," says Miles.

CITIZENS TRANSFER & STORAGE

The townspeople of Tucson viewed the arrival of the railroad in 1890 with grave suspicions. They stood before a belching machine on iron wheels that was a new Trojan horse in the heart of hard-won Tucson. But a quarter-century later it was generally agreed that this path to progress had not been a betrayal.

Citizens Transfer & Storage Co., Inc., is Tucson's oldest moving and storage company. Founded in 1907 by A.M. Franklin (as Citizen's Transfer Company), the enterprise was located at 24 North Stone (the present site of the Home Federal Tower).

With the railroad came building supplies, ready-made fashions, general commodities, ranch and farm supplies, and visitors from the East. Citizens Transfer Company delivered freight and baggage from the railroad depot to travelers and local businesses.

In 1920 John W. Archer bought the business, and shortly thereafter E.R. "Ed" Belton joined the company as a clerk. Belton, who graduated from the University of Arizona with a degree in business-commerce, became the secretary/treasurer of the newly incorporated Citizens Transfer & Storage Co., Inc., in 1923. In 1929 John Archer and Ed Belton completed a new warehouse at 44 West 6th Street with its own private rail siding. In that year Citizens Transfer became a charter member of Allied Van Lines, which would soon become the largest interstate moving company in America. The dramatic growth of the interstate moving business was stimulated by America's interstate highway system and a mobile corporate America.

John Archer passed away in 1952 and the business became entirely owned by the Belton family. At that time Ed Belton was named president. In 1956 Ed Belton's son, E.W. "Bill" Belton, joined the business as a mover. In 1981 grandson John E. Belton began working at the company during summer breaks from NAU. Recently, John was promoted to operations manager.

In 1985 Citizens Transfer & Storage Co., Inc., consolidated all local operations to its present location at 601 East 24th Street. The focus of the company has changed since the beginning years from local drayage and cartage to its current operation. During the 1930s the company also operated a wholesale beer and wine distributorship. In 1968 Citizens opened a branch office in Sierra Vista to serve the community and Fort Huachuca military post. Citizens Transfer formed a partnership in 1989 and bought Benton Moving Services, an Allied Van Lines agency in Albuquerque, New Mexico. The company is currently involved in all facets of moving, including local, interstate, and international relocations, as well as document and record storage and commercial warehousing.

E. W. "Bill" Belton, president, Citizens Transfer & Storage

After having been president of the company since 1952, Ed Belton died in 1984, and Bill Belton took over the responsibility of leadership of the company.

"Our industry has changed drastically over the years and we have kept abreast of those changes by our diversification of locations and services," says Bill Belton.

THE TUCSON CORK

The location of The Tucson Cork restaurant says a great deal about it. At the bend in the road where North Wilmot becomes East Tanque Verde, The Tucson Cork stands in the city's mainstream. Yet, removed from the busy thoroughfare by its own short, paved drive, it is also a place apart. Which is just how the countless, loyal patrons of The Tucson Cork over the past 30 years—some of them second-generation regulars—have felt about it. It's simply "The Cork," a special restaurant, a place apart from the rest.

There are many adjectives that can be used to describe The Cork. The first, as guests come up that short drive off Tanque Verde, is "inviting." An unpretentious yet dignified Spanish Colonial brick structure, The Cork might be mistaken for a residence in the foothills.

LEFT The Cork has a 20-item, garden-fresh salad bar.

Open the front door and enter, and the next adjective is "comfortable." From the trademark corner fireplace and the prompt greeting from the courteous staff, to the subtly separated, interwoven dining areas, The Cork represents friendliness. The decor is a unique blend of dark, gleaming wood, open-beam ceilings, saltillo tile floors, wrought iron fixtures, and Native American artifacts.

The third adjective is "excellent," for no other word describes the food at The Cork as well. Its reputation as one of Tucson's finest purveyors of steak dinners is richly deserved. The Cork's prime rib and steaks are all prime grade beef, and all servings are prime fillet cuts, each grilled to the diner's specifications.

But, as its patrons know, The Cork is not a one-dimensional "steak house." The menu—a hefty meat cleaver, another Cork tradition—is not only varied but health conscious.

"We know eating healthy is important to our customers, and it's important to us, too," says Bill Hillenbrand, who, with his wife, Doby, has owned The Tucson Cork for a decade.

Prominent on The Cork's menu are a fresh seafood catch-of-the-day, daily seafood specials, and Hawaiian chicken. The Cork's 20-item salad bar is garden fresh daily.

And speaking of popular, a unique house specialty at The Cork is buffalo. Supplied exclusively to The Cork from his brother Ray Hillenbrand's ranch in South Dakota, The Cork's buffalo steaks and prime rib have rapidly caught the attention of Tucson diners. With a taste similar to beef, yet pleasantly distinctive, buffalo is 98 percent lean and, while containing every bit as much protein as beef, is significantly lower in cholesterol and fat.

Inviting, comfortable, excellent . . . add to these words a final adjective: memorable. Once people dine at The Tucson Cork, they remember it and want to return.

BELOW The Cork has been a Tucson tradition for more than 30 years.

LOEWS VENTANA CANYON RESORT

The Spaniards named it Ventana (window)—describing the effect created by a large rock outcropping at the head of the canyon. Today that canyon and Tucson's magnificent 9,000-foot Santa Catalina Mountains form a dramatic backdrop for the Southwest's most distinctive destination resort, Loews Ventana Canyon Resort.

Sprawling across 94 acres in a giant saguaro forest, Loews Ventana Canyon Resort hugs the mountainside while blending with and preserving the Sonoran desert.

Environmental protection measures taken by Loews include preservation of half the 1,050-acre property as open space and retention of all mesquite trees and saguaro cactus. In fact, the resort's location was actually shifted from its original site to ensure the safety of a 300-year-old saguaro, one of 22,000 of the unique species of cactus that dot the nearby mountainside. A natural water course cascades down an 80-foot canyon wall to the resort's main entrance, where a dramatic 1.5- acre lake and tiered waterfall provide the ultimate challenge to golfers on the Canyon Course's famed 18th hole.

For two consecutive years Ventana Canyon has been the site of the nationally televised Merrill Lynch Shoot-Out. Golfers worldwide are now enjoying the experience of golf on the PGA, Fazio-designed, 18-hole Canyon Course at the resort.

RIGHT One of the Lakeside Spa and Tennis Club's attractions is a 50-foot lap pool and a Jacuzzi in a gorgeous, desert-fringed setting.

Adjacent to the Ventana Canyon Resort is the Lakeside Spa and Tennis Club, where a professional staff performs fitness training, massage therapy, private tennis lessons, aerobics instruction, and beauty salon services for men and women. In a spacious spa atmosphere surrounded by the desert and fringed with a mile-and-a-quarter jogging course, 10 tennis courts, a 50-foot lap pool, and a Jacuzzi, the lakeside area features wet and dry saunas, showers and locker rooms, Universal weight and exercise equipment, and a pro shop with sportswear and designer logo wear.

The Ventana Tennis Academy offers ongoing clinics for local players as well as two- and four-day all-inclusive packages for visitors. Recreation director Bill McGrath assists with local instruction. Together they bring the playing experience of world-ranked tennis players to the Tucson community.

Loews Ventana Canyon Resort offers 400 expansive and elegantly appointed guest rooms and suites—each with private balconies and spectacular views of the mountains or city. Additional amenities at the four-star hotel include four restaurants and lounges.

BELOW A 1.5-acre lake and tiered waterfall provide a beautiful backdrop for Canyon Course's famed 18th hole.

SUNDT CORP.

To many Tucsonans the name Sundt is synonymous with construction. For more than 60 years the Tucson-based family of companies has played a vital role in the city's evolution from a dusty desert outpost to the vibrant metropolis of today.

M.M. Sundt Construction Co. was founded in 1890 in neighboring New Mexico by Mauritz Martinsen Sundt, a Norwegian immigrant. In 1929 Sundt and his son, John, came to Tucson to build a Methodist church near the University of Arizona. In the tiny town John saw a future filled with promise, and decided to stay.

In 1936, with the country in the midst of the Great Depression, the University of Arizona began a major expansion of its Tucson campus. The goal was to provide much-needed facilities while at the same time stimulating the depressed local economy. Funds for the program came from the Public Works Administration.

M.M. Sundt was awarded a contract for six of the projects, which were constructed simultaneously: a women's physical education building, ROTC stables, an infirmary, the original chemistry/ physics building, the original administration building, and the UA auditorium (now called Centennial Hall). From that period forward, the UA's expansion plans frequently included Sundt.

During the 1960s the UA continued to expand, and the company constructed many new buildings including the science library, the civil engineering building, the pharmacy-microbiology building, the new administration building, and the modern languages building. Campus projects completed by Sundt during the 1970s include the new library, the College of Law building, and the McKale Memorial Center.

The McKale Memorial Center was named for J.F. (Pop) McKale, the UA's late athletic director and longtime coach. The center was built by M.M. Sundt Construction Co. at an approximate cost of $8.15 million. Covering about two acres, McKale is the second-largest building on the UA campus, exceeded in size only by the University Medical Center.

Company president Bob Sundt said McKale's unusual roof was constructed on the ground, then raised into position. First roof trusses, bracing, catwalks, lights, and mechanical ductwork were erected on the ground. This assembly was jacked up 28 feet, where part of the truss extensions were installed and welded. The roof was then jacked up another 30 feet to

ABOVE The project to construct skyboxes on the west side of Arizona Stadium presented some unique construction challenges for Sundt.

LEFT UA Scholarship Suites were completed by Sundt just in time for the 1989 Wildcat football season opener.

its final position 58 feet above the ground. The truss extensions were then completed, the $100,000 copper fascia installed, and the roof insulation and covering placed.

After two years of construction McKale Memorial Center opened in February 1973.

Driven by the need to replace Arizona Stadium's outdated press box, rated as one of the poorest in the Pac-10 Conference, and the demonstrated marketing potential of "skyboxes" for devoted Wildcat football fans, the UA Foundation undertook a challenging project. Officially known as "Scholarship Suites," the project was completed by Sundt just in time for the 1989 Wildcat season opener against Stanford on September 2. The Scholarship Suites project elevated the school's press box from the cellar to the top of the Pac-10. Profits from lease of the facilities are used by the foundation for academic and athletic scholarships.

In addition to the new press box (renamed the Media Center) the four-level project provides 25 suites, a loge area with 327 sheltered seats, and reception and viewing areas for the school's president and the intercollegiate athletics director.

The loge seating is on the first, or lowest, level. The second and third levels contain 25 individual suites and the President's Suite, which takes up what would have been five individual suite modules. The Media Center takes up all of the fourth level.

Sundt started the project on September 15, 1988. Limited construction continued throughout the football season, as Sundt pressed ahead with as much work as it could accomplish while the stadium was still in use. The last home game was played on November 26 against archrival Arizona State University. Fifteen days later portions of the existing press box were removed.

BELOW The construction of McKale Memorial Center was one of more than 50 projects Sundt has completed to date on the UA campus.

The skybox project was placed on a six-day work week in early December 1988; five months later the steel erector was placed on a double-shift basis. This double shift enabled the skybox construction to be completed in time for the opening football game of the 1989 season.

The association of Sundt and the University of Arizona is one of long-standing. To date, Sundt Corp. has completed more than 50 projects on the UA campus. It's a simple matter of symbiosis. Sundt keeps promises, meets deadlines, stays under budget, does good quality work and plays fair.

INTERGROUP HEALTHCARE CORPORATION

Intergroup Healthcare Corporation began in 1981 as Intergroup of Arizona, Inc. The company had a single product—Intergroup HMO—and a simple idea: to provide quality health care at an affordable price.

From that simple idea, Intergroup has grown to become one of Arizona's largest and one of the country's fastest growing full-service managed health care companies.

The company has received numerous accolades along the way. In 1987 and 1988, *Inc.* magazine ranked Intergroup of Arizona as one of the fastest growing privately held companies in the country.

In 1990 Intergroup of Arizona was invited to join The HMO Group, a prestigious national alliance of 18 independent group practice HMOs from around the country.

In the late 1980s, while other HMOs suffered financial losses, Intergroup of Arizona's solid management and stability kept it financially prosperous.

With this history of success for its foundation, Intergroup made a transition to Intergroup Healthcare Corporation in 1991. In August of that year, the company completed an initial public offering of 3.25 million shares of common stock that generated net proceeds of $42.9 million.

Prior to the initial public offering, Intergroup HMO was completely owned by the physicians of Thomas-Davis Medical Center (TDMC), Arizona's oldest and largest multi-specialty group practice. (After the initial public offering, TDMC retained approximately 67 percent of Intergroup Healthcare Corporation.)

Throughout the company's history, physicians have been actively involved in management and planning. This physician orientation helps ensure Intergroup's emphasis remains on quality health care. At the same time, risk-sharing arrangements and other financial incentives encourage the appropriate use of medical services.

ABOVE Rick Barrett is president and chief executive officer of Intergroup Healthcare Corporation.

LEFT Wilber C. Voss, M.D., is the company's chairman of the board.

In addition to growing in size and stature, Intergroup Health Care Corporation has several companies under its umbrella. Intergroup the HMO remains the largest and now includes an HMO product for Medicare subscribers called Seniorcare. There are several other companies as well. Under Bay Colony, IGHC offers three product lines: point of service, preferred provider and indemnity insurance options. Intercare is a third-party administrator for employers who self -insure their health care, while AHCCCS select offers coverage for Arizona's Medicaid population.

THE WESTIN LA PALOMA

The Westin La Paloma is more than a world-class resort. It is a sports enthusiast's dream. Guests of The Westin La Paloma have the best of two worlds: a complete complement of activities at the main resort building, plus access to all the services and recreational options of one of the finest private country clubs in the nation.

The 27-hole Jack Nicklaus Signature golf course, named one of the top 75 resort courses in the country by *Golf Digest* magazine, completely surrounds the resort complex. Play is exclusive to club members and resort guests. The championship course offers year-round golfing amidst high desert terrain. Jack Nicklaus' unique design offers guests a choice in their level of challenge. Each hole has four or five tee boxes.

ABOVE **W**estin La Paloma's free-form pool features the cool convenience of a swim-up bar.

BELOW **T**he 27-hole Jack Nicklaus Signature golf course completely surrounds the resort complex.

The three nines of the golf course are named for the types of terrain they traverse: Hill, Ridge, and Canyon, and are designed to be fun for both occasional golfers and low handicap players, but still be suitable for tournament play. The landscape incorporates natural desert vegetation, including hundreds of giant saguaro cacti.

The 35,000-square-foot clubhouse is in easy walking distance of guest room buildings. The clubhouse includes a pro shop, men's and women's locker rooms, the La Paloma dining room, and the 19th Hole Lounge.

But there is more to the resort than golf. The La Paloma Country Club Tennis and Health facilities boasts a total of 12 championship tennis courts, including four Georgia clay courts and eight hardcourt surface courts. Ten are lighted for night play. The complex has been named one of the top 50 in the country by *Tennis* magazine.

Other athletic amenities include a free-form swimming pool with waterslide and swim-up bar, plus a lagoon with a waterfall and beaches. Also on the premises are three therapeutic spas, a sand volleyball court, a croquet lawn, and jogging and cycling trails. The Children's Lounge offers year-round supervised fun for kids six months to 12 years of age.

The Westin La Paloma health club features indoor racquetball and an ongoing selection of aerobics classes. The weight room is fully equipped with the latest Nautilus equipment.

For the ultimate in individual attention, the Personal Services Center offers massage, body wraps, and extensive skin care and cosmetic services.

The Westin La Paloma has 487 guest rooms located in 27 complexes arranged in a village setting. Each accommodation features its own private balcony or patio, spacious sitting area, separate shower and tub, and an oversized closet and wardrobe. Many of the suites include wood burning fireplaces, sunken spa tubs, service bars, and conference tables.

Of course, a cornucopia of unparalleled dining experiences are available at The Westin La Paloma, including everything from fine country club dining to a quick, casual bite.

For discriminating travelers, and particularly sports enthusiasts, The Westin La Paloma Resort is a natural.

REHAB INSTITUTE OF TUCSON

Thanks to medical science, more people are surviving critical injuries that at one time would have been fatal. More people are living longer, but the disabling effects of severe injuries and the aging process require rehabilitation.

In response to a growing need for intensive rehabilitation programs, Rehab Institute of Tucson opened in July 1990 and is now accredited by both JCAHO and CARF. The comprehensive medical rehabilitation facility, which is spread over 7.55 acres adjacent to Tucson Medical Center, is the first freestanding hospital in southern Arizona dedicated entirely to rehabilitation. Outreach and educational programs also serve the rural areas of the state and northern Mexico.

"A successful rehabilitation program promotes self-esteem and independence for the patient and involves them and their families as integral members of the theraputic team" says Barbara Giesser, M.D., Medical Director, "Our ultimate goal is to integrate patients back into their community."

Well over 80 percent of the patients served by Rehab Institute of Tucson return home, as opposed to being placed in a nursing home or dependent living situation. This is higher than the national average.

The institute brings a valued medical resource to the residents of southern Arizona. It offers the latest, most technologically advanced equipment and is staffed by highly trained medical professionals. The facility can serve up to 80 inpatients and offers outpatient and full-day treatment programs.

"Rehabilitation" is the process of building a new beginning for the individual disabled by accident or illness. Rehab Institute of Tucson has developed specialized programs for stroke, neurological disorders, arthritis, brain injury, orthopedics, spinal cord injury, adaptive driving, and return to work. Programs are also available for pediatrics and amputees.

Specialized programs with interdisciplinary teams tailor services to meet the needs and goals of each individual patient.

"The focus of rehabilitation medicine is to maximize functional independence within the limitations imposed by disabilities." says Giesser, "We give people back their futures."

Services available at Rehab Institute of Tucson include physical, speech and occupational therapies; psychology; respiratory therapy; bilingual services; biofeedback; computerized cognitive rehab; attention process training; and support groups and activities therapy. Community Rehabilitation Services, another Rehab Systems Company program, provides a continuum of care in transitioning brain-injured patients home and into the community.

Rehab Institute of Tucson is one of 12 facilities operated by Rehab Systems Company, a NovaCare Operating Company.

ABOVE Full-day treatment programs enable patients to live at home while receiving comprehensive services.

BELOW Rehab Institute of Tucson is southern Arizona's first freestanding medical rehabilitation facility.

MILLER BROS.

When Duane and Cecil Miller formed a partnership in 1948 for the purpose of leasing and farming an 80-acre summer crop of grain, it was not in their wildest dreams what kind of company Miller Bros. would become nearly a half-century later.

The Miller brothers were raised, educated (both graduated from the UA), and worked in the livestock and farming industries. From their initial investment in that first crop, they expanded their interests until they were ranching in northern Arizona and farming and operating feedlots in the Salt River Valley. In the northern half of Arizona, there were few ranches the Millers had not purchased cattle from. They had long associations with the state's leading ranchers, including the Kieckhefer, Babbitt, Cowden, Greenway, Stewart and Pollock families.

LEFT Duane Miller, president of Foothills Real Estate Investments, Inc.

In 1973, because of the state of the Arizona economy at the time, the Miller brothers began to divest themselves of ranches and farms through trades and sales. From ranching and farming Miller Bros. turned to real estate, subdivisions, recreational activities and commercial realty.

During that period Miller Bros. owned office buildings and shopping centers. The firm also developed private, security-guarded subdivisions, using its own contracting company.

Today the business is operated under the divisions of Millco Contracting Co., Foothills Real Estate & Investments, Inc. (with five branch offices), Sedona Racquet Club, Inc., and Foothills South.

Befitting the company's roots, Miller Bros. still maintains the Coconino Cattle Co. and the Miller Bros.-D.K. Ranch with a herd of registered Saler Cattle. The company also has a small farm on the scenic Oak Creek in the Verde Valley and a ranch near Flagstaff.

Cecil Miller could not quite disassociate himself from farming and operates several farms in California. Duane Miller is president of Foothills Real Estate Investments, Inc., which is headquartered in Sedona, Arizona.

Today Foothills Real Estate and Investments, Inc., operates general real estate, residential property management, commercial property management and development of real estate properties.

Foothills Real Estate & Investments, Inc., has been providing professional real estate services in Arizona since 1972. In two decades it has grown with the state to become the largest independently owned real estate company in northern Arizona.

Foothills has earned a reputation for excellence in its field due to a commitment to quality service provided by professionals trained and experienced in all aspects of real estate.

"Foothills recognizes the real estate investment as the most important investment most people make," says Duane Miller.

Miller Bros. has come a long way from farming a summer crop in 1948 to where its operations are today, and the future of the company is as bright as the Arizona sun.

BELOW Broadway Plaza is owned and managed by Foothills Real Estate in Tucson.

THOMAS-DAVIS MEDICAL CENTERS

Today, more than 70 years after first opening its doors in Tucson, Thomas-Davis Medical Centers continues to lead the way with contemporary health services blended with a "tradition of caring" that Arizona families have depended upon since 1920.

The heart of the Thomas-Davis Medical Centers (TDMC) health care delivery system is the multispecialty group practice concept. By offering care in virtually every medical specialty and offering comprehensive ancillary and support services, including urgent care treatment, the physicians and staff at TDMC can literally provide a lifetime of care for any patient.

ABOVE Thomas-Davis central facility in Tucson

Many patients choose their doctor and stay with that physician, based upon a feeling or sense of caring conveyed by the doctor. TDMC physicians have earned a reputation for building trust and confidence among their patients.

TDMC has earned a reputation for responsiveness to patients' needs for convenient accessible care. As Tucson has grown, the center has opened satellite facilities that are conveniently located in each quadrant of the city. The growing community of Green Valley now has a full-service TDMC location to serve area residents.

In 1984 Thomas-Davis Medical Centers expanded to Maricopa County by opening a clinic in Tempe. During the past few years Thomas-Davis has greatly expanded its service in the Phoenix area. In 1990 facilities were opened in Phoenix, Scottsdale, Glendale, Chandler, Ahwatukee and Moon Valley.

As time and convenience grow ever more important to busy families, TDMC continues to respond by offering after-hours urgent care at four of its facilities. Outpatient surgery is performed at TDMC's state-of-the-art Surgi-Center, allowing patients the comfort and cost-effectiveness of minor surgery without hospitalization.

In the mid-1980s TDMC enhanced its health care services for women. The TDMC Women's Center opened in 1987, providing an attractive, comfortable environment where women can confer with specialists in obstetrics and gynecology. Education classes, nutrition counseling and many other specialized services are provided at this convenient, private facility.

All centers statewide provide both fee-for-service medical care as well as managed health care services.

Thomas-Davis Medical Centers is committed to quality patient care, something that can happen only when a physician and patient come together in a caring and professional environment.

RUSSETT SOUTHWEST CORPORATION

Heating and cooling was a different business when Russett started in 1947. All that was needed then were employees with sound mechanical knowledge and a willingness to work.

Skyrocketing utility rates and finite environmental resources have changed all that. Russett's years of knowledge and testing have been adapted to successful technological advancements that can now keep comfort at a reasonable cost, while also being in harmony with environmental limitations.

LEFT Russett Southwest Corporation installs heating and cooling systems that are economical and energy efficient.

"Russett is very concerned with the conservation of natural resources. We did a lot of research and development last year," says Gary Gibson, president and chief executive officer. Russett Southwest Corp., a privately held corporation, is owned by the Gibson family. His wife, Kathleen, and two sons, Phillip and Shawn, also work for Russett, as does his son-in-law, Jimmy Baldwin.

Russett Southwest has the advanced training to deal with entire systems: heating, air conditioning, evaporative cooling, special accessories and sophisticated controls. They are skilled in delivering maximum comfort with minimum use of gas and electricity.

According to Gibson, the average house wastes at least 30 percent of its heating and cooling energy due to improper construction methods.

Russett has developed a whole new concept of how people can be comfortable within their chosen setting. Through a highly developed, sophisticated computer imaging system, Russett Southwest can analyze how the unseen aspects of a structure's construction affects operating costs and comfortability.

Important aspects to consider are window glass; construction of walls, ceiling and roof; what type and application of insulation is best; and the thermal efficiency of building materials. Because insulation is one of the key elements in efficiency, Russett has recently opened a new division that will install only residential housing insulation.

"We try to stay ahead of everyone in the industry with new products and new innovations," says Gibson.

Whether building a home or simply updating the comfort systems, Russett uses their applied technology to get the most out of the whole system.

Adhering to a hard policy of not installing anyone else's design, Russett engineers and designs the system's duct work, insulation, registers and equipment selection.

"We have to live with what we do," says Gibson. "My theory is that if it works on paper, it will work when installed."

Russett focuses on the consumer so that customers can make an informed choice about what they want in a heating and cooling system.

Complying with local codes does not ensure energy efficiency. The only thing that guarantees energy efficiency is the quality of the installing contractor. Russett Southwest offers consumers complete comfort while being in harmony with their environment.

BELOW Russett Southwest systems deliver the maximum comfort to any environment.

CYCARE SYSTEMS

While the nation worries about the escalating cost of health care, a company headquartered in Scottsdale has a solution. CyCare Systems is one of America's leading providers of information management systems and services to the medical group practice industry.

According to Jim H. Houtz, chairman, chief executive officer, and founder of CyCare Systems, manipulation of information (what is called clerical medicine) represents a significant portion of the nation's health care tab.

Founded by Houtz in 1967 in Dubuque, Iowa, as Computer Consulting Service, CyCare currently employs more than 1,100 people in 15 offices across the country. CyCare serves more than 4,800 clients nationwide, ringing up sales of nearly $80 million annually.

From the beginning, Houtz pinpointed that the processing of information for the health care industry would be CyCare's niche. He quickly established a policy of acquiring small regional firms that would aid him in both serving and seeking his chosen client base. By the time the company went public in 1981, CyCare was writing software and reselling hardware.

The first vendor to offer patient scheduling and a full range of processing options, CyCare soon developed a broad marketing base. By 1984 the firm was growing at an annual rate of 37 percent. Today CyCare is the leading provider of business management solutions to the health care industry. The company's clients are large medical group practices, physicians and dentists, and hospital-based physicians.

The health care industry depends upon CyCare to provide computerized management information systems that improve physician productivity, decrease costs, and increase cash flow. The systems and services provided by CyCare allow physicians to better focus on the practice of medicine, while creating a superior business environment for their practices.

ABOVE Jim H. Houtz (left), chairman and CEO, and Raymond R. Maturi, president and COO.

LEFT More than 25,000 physicians rely on CyCare's Systems' services each day.

CyCare provides business solutions through the application of software systems such as accounting and billing, electronic claims clearing, patient registration and scheduling, prepaid health care, and third-party management. CyCare will also educate and train clients' key staff members, thereby improving productivity and administrative management. This ultimately results in assisting the health care industry to improve the quality of patient care.

CyCare's innovative electronic claims processing system allows clients to submit health insurance claims in a common format. CyCare then edits and reformats these claims to carrier specifications and submits them directly to the carrier electronically or on paper. Today, CyCare processes more electronic medical claims for physician services than any other company in the industry.

As a pioneer and market leader in effective information management systems to medical group practices, CyCare is an important business partner to America's health care industry.

WEISER LOCK

Weiser Lock relocated its manufacturing facility from Southern California to Tucson in January 1990 and hired more than 400 workers from the Tucson area. One year later Weiser decided to also move its administrative and marketing activities out of California and onto the Tucson site, creating another 50 jobs. The plant now employs more than 500 and utilizes some of the most modern equipment and manufacturing techniques in the world today.

Weiser Lock also has plants in Europe, Thailand and Canada. The Tucson facility is the only one in the United States, and is also the company's largest plant.

Weiser Lock was established in 1904 by the Weiser family. Operating as a foundry in South Gate, California, the company specialized in hardware and custom, ornate locks. Other items made by Weiser included door knockers, hammered hinge straps, letter box plates, coat hooks and handrail brackets.

By the mid-1920s Weiser had moved into a larger facility and begun to manufacture an extensive line of hardware for builders. During World War II, with the supply of raw materials restricted, the company contracted to produce aircraft parts and continued to grow and improve the business.

In 1946 the decision was made to resume the manufacture of locks. Weiser's new vision included the commitment to manufacture only one line of residential locks—the best.

From the beginning Weiser products were welcomed into the market by builders who were impressed by the company's commitment to quality. Tremendous growth occurred during the 1940s and 1950s as customers noted with satisfaction that Weiser's sales force was more than willing to help them solve their problems as well as sell them products.

ABOVE Weiser Lock opened its 240,000-square-foot facility in Tucson in January of 1990.

RIGHT Weiser Lock began its operations in 1904 manufacturing various hardware such as custom ornate locks, door knockers, letter box plates, and coat hooks.

LEFT Weiser Lock's Tucson plant utilizes some of the most modern equipment and manufacturing technology.

Weiser Lock was purchased by Norris Industries in 1967, and Norris Industries was purchased by Masco Corporation in 1985. A *Fortune* 250 company, Masco Corporation is one of the country's largest manufacturers of brand-name consumer products for the home.

During both acquisitions, Weiser remained strong in the builders' hardware marketplace, continuing to develop new products and expand into the retail market. Today Weiser's Tucson plant produces and distributes all the Weiser locks sold in the United States.

The company's strength is its people. Weiser has proven that talented people, given the proper environment to perform at their full potential, produce outstanding and superior results.

With the move to Tucson completed, Weiser is poised to go after a greater market share and continue its quest for excellence. With a core of dedicated people, the company is more committed than ever to producing a quality product at a competitive price and supplying it to all customers in a timely manner.

WESTWARD LOOK RESORT

The Westward Look Resort has been offering its services to Tucson's visitors for more than 50 years. Located in the foothills of the Santa Catalina Mountains on 80 acres, the premier resort has a long history rich with western tradition.

In 1912 William and Maria Watson purchased a 172-acre homestead above the small city of Tucson. Desiring a traditional southwestern-style adobe home, the couple employed a well-known architect named Starkweather. This brilliant designer cleverly disguised the concrete and steel building to appear to be constructed of the mud and straw adobe bricks. Other prominent features are the stone hearth located in what is presently known as the Vigas Conference room, the Ponderosa pine ceiling beams that were harvested on the higher ridges of the nearby mountains, and ocotillo branches used on the veranda ceiling for their natural ability to resist weathering.

ABOVE One of several guest room complexes.

By 1930 there were 15 guest cottages located on the property, and the roots of the Westward Look Resort were established. During the 1940s the Nason family purchased the land from the Watsons, eventually expanded to 55 rooms, and operated the property as a Western guest ranch complete with stables and horses.

In 1972 a local entrepreneur, Jack Hoag, purchased the resort. Realizing the potential for a truly great resort, he spent the next 10 years expanding. In 1982 RKO purchased the then 160-room resort and over the next three years modernized and expanded further.

Westward Look Resort now offers 244 extra-large rooms, including 10 full suites. Each room has a private entrance, balcony or patio, cable television and movies, AM/FM stereo, coffee/tea service, mini-refrigerator and tabletop ironing board with iron.

Available to Westward Look guests is a recreation center that includes eight championship Laykold tennis courts, a lap pool, a weight and exercise room, and a pro shop. *Tennis* magazine perennially rates the Westward Look as one of the top 50 tennis resorts in the nation.

The resort also maintains a sports park that features a baseball diamond, basketball and volleyball courts, shuffleboard, and horseshoe pits. A jogging trail winds through cacti and other natural vegetation.

For more than 20 years the Gold Room has been recognized as one of Tucson's finest dining rooms. The resort also has a casual Lobby Cafe, poolside cabanas for grilled sandwiches and beverages, and room service.

The Lookout Lounge, with a great view of the city lights, offers live entertainment, seasonal "Sports Mondays," and jazz concerts.

The resort's name, "Westward Look," was borrowed from the nineteenth-century English poet, Arthur Hugh Clough: "In front, the sun climbs slow, how slowly. But Westward, look, the land is bright."

WORK RECOVERY, INC.

Figuring out just what kinds of physical tasks employees can handle has never been easy. But the Ergos Work Simulator from Work Recovery, Inc., can assess the physical capabilities of workers and guide employers when determining whether an injured employee should return to work or whether a prospective employee should be hired.

Ergos is a computer-controlled collection of switches, levers, colorful balls and heavy weights that keeps a person busy at various tasks for about four hours. The system measures 28 variables of strength, dexterity and flexibility and compares them to standards generated by government agencies and private time-motion studies.

Ergos tests up to five people at once. It begins by asking a person to choose from its data base of 14,000 occupations. Drawing on that data base, the machine duplicates the physical movements required. These can be modified by the physical evaluator who oversees the operation if the task being tested for differs from the norm.

The goal of some Ergos tests is obvious, such as the strength measurements involved in gripping a bar and pushing, pulling, or lifting it. But many tasks are intricate and it isn't readily apparent what's being tested. People must put colored balls into a basket, carry it up some steps and put the balls into a hole in the machine, for example.

As a person works, the test administrator observes and enters information into the computer by passing an electronic wand over a bar code associated with a specific comment, which might say "the evaluee demonstrated facial grimacing" or "the evaluee was cooperative but displayed some hesitancy."

"The bar code system of notemaking greatly speeds evaluation and avoids mistakes," explains Tom Brandon, founder and president of Work Recovery, Inc.

Ergos is designed to spot inconsistencies. For instance, a person who appears to be unable to lift more than four pounds in the first obvious test of strength may lift and carry 10 pounds of colorful balls without realizing what they are doing.

"Someone may be able to manipulate the system for 30 minutes or even an hour, but when you have them doing tasks for three or four hours, they cannot consistently manipulate the system," says Brandon.

At the end of an Ergos session, the system churns out a detailed evaluation of a person's ability to do a variety of tasks. It also points out performance inconsistencies that could indicate malingering. The reports are written in non-judgmental, objective prose that leaves it to a physician, employer, or others to draw conclusions.

Brandon and his partner, chief executive officer Stephen Bubala, each owned and operated successful companies in the vocational/medical testing field for more than two decades before forming Work Recovery Inc., in 1987.

SOUTHWEST HAZARD CONTROL, INC.

Southwest Hazard Control, Inc. (SHC), begun in 1982, is an Arizona-based corporation whose purpose is to solve environmental concerns for its clients in an efficient, effective and ethical manner. This process is innovative, dynamic and satisfying for everyone, both professionally and financially.

The company is a financially sound, growth-oriented environmental remediation company, founded by Gerald J. Karches, a physicist and industrial hygienist. The staff applies innovative procedures to solve environmental problems for current and future clients. SHC treats its clients as the reason for its existence and its employees as a team, for the benefit of all concerned. Its employees strive to be the best there are in solving environmental issues in a safe and effective manner before these issues become real hazards. They also actively promote sound environmental practice within the community. SHC's goal is to do it right the first time, on time, within budget and as planned. SHC is licensed in Arizona, New Mexico, Nevada, California.

The operating resources at SHC consist of two major divisions: asbestos abatement and hazardous waste management.

To date the asbestos abatement division has completed more than 2,000 asbestos abatement projects. The jobs range in size from $500 to $1.7 million. SHC clients include private residences, schools, hospitals, power plants, mines, government (federal, state, and local), military bases, shopping centers, and other commercial facilities. It has a certified laboratory to analyze bulk and air samples for asbestos.

ABOVE Asbestos technicians at work.

BELOW Hazardous materials view of SHC.

Hazardous waste is defined by the EPA as "any substance that when released into the environment may present substantial danger to public health, welfare, or the environment." Typically these wastes include corrosives, heavy metals, pesticides, PCBs, toxic chemicals, explosives, and flammables.

The Hazardous Waste Management (HAZMAT) division provides services to determine if hazardous substances are present, the extent or severity of the contamination or concentration, and what remedial actions should be taken. The trained staff also provides corrective actions that may be necessary to bring the client into compliance with regulations. This includes lab packing, neutralizing, bioremediation, or shipping waste for recycling, incineration, or land filling. Over 300 HAZMAT projects have been successfully completed.

Safety of its workers is SHC's first priority, and protecting its clients and the environment is its mission. Southwest Hazard Control, Inc., would like to help solve your environmental concerns.

JUDITH ABRAMS & ASSOCIATES, INC.

A successful businessperson once said that location was everything to his company. Not so for a consulting firm. Reputation is everything when a company's services include maintaining a pulse on community interests, issues, and trends, and developing effective communications strategies.

The principal in Judith Abrams & Associates has built a solid reputation in all sectors of Arizona's economy, particularly in southern Arizona and Phoenix. In an independent survey of local news media, Judith Abrams & Associates was rated the most competent public relations firm in Tucson.

Abrams has made it her business to know community leaders, including businesspeople, government officials, educators, journalists and community activists.

"As full-service consultants we provide advice on community trends and issues, as well as organizing people and ideas into a plan of action. JA&A understands how organizations, from the very large to the very small, function. We can then interact with all levels of operation," says Judith K. Abrams, president and founder of the business.

"We also provide extensive expertise for developing communications tools for clients—whether their needs include preparing an annual report, a press release, internal employee meetings, a company announcement, meetings with editorial boards, newsletters, government proposals, the opening of a new business, or government relations," she says.

Since the firm was launched in 1983, Abrams has worked with some of Tucson's top employers and has tackled major issues relating to community growth, transportation, the environment and education. Projects JA&A have worked on include the site selection for the Main Library downtown, the ownership and name change for the original Levy's department store, the groundbreaking for the United Bank Tower (now known as the Citibank Building), the Spare the Air clean air campaign, McCulloch's introduction and move to Tucson, and the opening of the Tucson Children's Museum.

Throughout the years the firm has worked with more than 50 Tucson companies and organizations. Longtime clients include Cooke CableVision, Tucson Realty and Trust Co., Tucson Osteopathic Medical Foundation, Westinghouse Communities, and Arizona Portland Cement.

Abrams brings to the firm's clients her extensive knowledge of the community and valuable personal contacts. She was chairman of the advisory committee to the Arizona Office of Tourism and worked for U.S. Senator Dennis DeConcini for more than 12 years. Abrams also served as a member of the U.S. Small Business Administration National Advisory Council.

Judith Abrams & Associates is the Tucson member of the Ruder/Finn Public Relations Network.

RIGHT Judith Abrams

ARIZONA ALUMNI ASSOCIATION

The Arizona Alumni Association is in the business of building relationships that last a lifetime.

When the Alumni Association was organized in 1897, its membership included all six people who had received degrees from the University of Arizona. To round out the membership roster, the 14 members of the UA faculty were made honorary alumni.

A quarter of a century later, UA alumni numbered more than 800, and the Alumni Association had its first permanent administrative office on campus, located in the Agriculture Building.

Today the Alumni Association generates involvement among its 140,000 members through strong club programs, college councils, and offices in Phoenix and Los Angeles. Its administrative offices are in the new UA Foundation/Alumni building at Speedway and Cherry.

There has been an enduring relationship between the Alumni Association and the UA Athletic Department. During the 1927-1928 school year, the association undertook its first fund-raising project. The campaign, headed by Ralph W. Bilby and A. Louis Slonaker, raised $100,000 for the construction of a new football stadium and athletic facilities. Arizona Stadium was dedicated on October 12, 1929, with Alumni Association president Harold G. Wilson presiding.

The UA's yearly homecoming weekend is the third-oldest such event in the nation, and homecoming is one of the Arizona Alumni Association's most visible events. Thousands of former students and others converge on campus for seminars, art shows, open houses, a festive party under colorful canopies on the UA's grassy mall, reunions of classes and athletic teams, dances, and other events.

RIGHT The new University of Arizona Foundation/Alumni Building is on the northwest corner of Speedway Boulevard and Cherry Avenue. Alumni from all over the country are trying to raise $2.5 million to name the building in honor of former UA vice president and honorary letterman Marvin D. "Swede" Johnson. Photo by Rochlin/Lester

In 1992 there were about 100 different events on the official Homecoming program and scores of "unofficial" activities. Almost 58,000 Wildcat fans jammed Arizona stadium for the Homecoming game.

During the year the Association assists in conducting the annual letterwinners breakfasts and the reunions for former football and basketball players.

To stay in touch with alumni, the Association produces a large number of publications, including the award winning *Arizona Alumnus* magazine. It also sponsors a monthly television program, "Arizona Alumni Forum" which airs on the ABC affiliates in Tucson and Phoenix.

Among the many ways the Association serves the U of A is through its state relations program in which Alumni keep the importance of the U of A on legislators' minds all year long.

The Association offers a wide range of other services to its members including educational travel, social and business networking opportunities, and a career connection service.

People who want to get in touch can take advantage of the country's most memorable toll-free number: 1-800-BEAT-ASU!

LEFT Wildcat hoop heroes from the early years gather at the Alumni Association's annual basketball reunion. Members of the emeritus team attending the 1991 reunion were: (back row, from left) Ray Naegle, Denny Jordan, Dave McMillen, Keith Mets, Carl Cameron, (middle row, from l.) Marion Beaver, Charles Walters, Tom Greenfield, Walter Helm, Neil Goodman, (front row, from l.) Pat Turner, Frank Davis, Dwayne Robinson, Dan Clarke, R.T. Gridley, and Earl Gieseke. Photo by Jon Alquist

CAT TRACKS

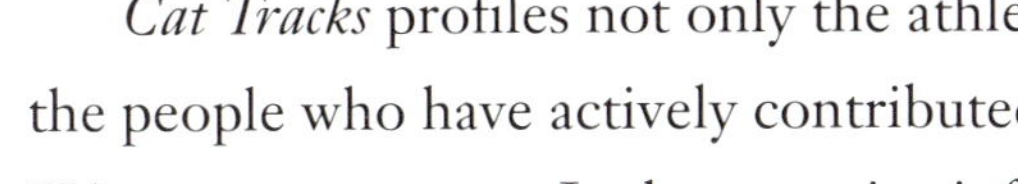

When Doug Carr decided to publish *Cat Tracks* in the spring of 1989, he was fulfilling a lifelong dream. "I wanted to get involved in sports and make money at it," says Carr, a diehard Wildcat basketball follower.

Carr has undertaken the ultimate challenge: To turn out a good product, to give people what they want, to represent UA in a classy manner—and still turn a profit.

Cat Tracks: The University of Arizona Sports Weekly gives its readers a close-up of the Wildcats with lively game-day coverage of UA games featuring exciting action photos. *Cat Tracks* covers all UA sports with feature looks at present athletes, a look back at former athletes, and a peek into the future of incoming recruits.

Steve Kerr, the 1988 Final Four team captain, contributes a humorous and colorful biweekly column titled "Inside the NBA." Larry Donald, publisher of *Basketball Times*, often contributes a column with his commentary on basketball from a national perspective.

"Our articles let the fans get to know the players, the coaches, and everyone involved with the UA sports programs," says Carr.

Cat Tracks profiles not only the athletes, but the people who have actively contributed to the UA sports programs. It also contains informative stories about Wildcat athletic facilities.

"*Cat Tracks* covers all University of Arizona sports," says Carr. "We emphasize the most popular sports, but we also devote space to the nonrevenue and club sports."

Cat Tracks captures the excitement of Arizona football, basketball and baseball, but doesn't neglect women's basketball, volleyball, or softball.

Cat Tracks uses a number of contributing writers, most of them UA students in the school of journalism. Production of the publication is done in-house on Macintosh computers and state-of-the-art support equipment.

Cat Tracks' cover features the UA colors of navy and cardinal in combination with a distinctive Wildcat paw print and innovative graphics or photography.

Cat Tracks is a totally positive publication catering to Wildcat enthusiasts everywhere. Local fans as well as alumni and friends outside the area can closely follow their favorite UA team in *Cat Tracks*.

pring, summer, fall, or winter, *Cat Tracks* is on the scene to cover all UA Sports.

All photos by James Orchard.

THE ARIZONA DAILY WILDCAT

The *Arizona Daily Wildcat* has been the voice of the students at the University of Arizona since 1899. Beginning as a monthly journal called *Sage Green and Silver*, the periodical has become the eighth-largest circulated collegiate daily newspaper in the United States. It is the seventh-largest newspaper in Arizona.

The publications of those early years were similar to UA campus life at the time: simple, homey and personal. Their pages were filled with sports news, gossip, jokes, society tidbits and praises for UA and its inhabitants. However, the writers and editors took their campus role seriously, and the issues they addressed are still a part of today's *Wildcat*: student control and self-government, rising costs, and national concerns that affect students as people.

The 1915-1916 school year saw the birth of the *Arizona Wildcat* when Orville "Speedy" McPherson, a bold liberal arts student and publication staff member, decided that UA needed an official weekly student mouthpiece. Finding administrators unwilling to finance the shaky venture, McPherson deposited $100 of his own money in the Southern Arizona Bank to cover expenses. He also chose the name that would stay with the paper.

The *Wildcat* had no office and little funding by the Associated Students, but it flourished. When McPherson graduated, his enthusiasm and advertising hustle left a lucrative newspaper, which the university then took over.

In 1935 the UA established a minor degree in journalism, and in 1940, a major. The *Wildcat* became an official laboratory for journalism classes, and students received a tough but excellent baptism in print, which eventually gained nationwide attention for UA and for the newspaper.

Production technology has changed greatly since the *Arizona Daily Wildcat* began publication in 1965. What has not changed throughout the years is the paper's quality and dedication.

Publication of the *Arizona Daily Wildcat* was announced in 1965, with advertising revenue paying for 85 percent of its operations costs. The remaining budget came from ASUA's student activity fees. The aggressive new daily publication was feeling the need to break free from outside influences, and a year later the relationship between the Journalism Department and the *Wildcat* was officially severed.

Today the *Arizona Daily Wildcat* is a strong independent newspaper. Operating within the UA Department of Student Publications, which also publishes the *Desert Yearbook*, the paper receives no funding from the university. It is entirely supported by advertising sold by student sales representatives. Ranking among the top 10 college newspapers nationwide in terms of circulation, news content, advertising inches, and payroll, the *Arizona Daily Wildcat* stands as a prominent and valued asset to Tucson and the University of Arizona community.

940/KNST-AM 93.7/KRQ-FM

Beginning in the spring of 1987 KNST's Sports Tonight had attracted enough audience participation to establish a consistent and lively sports-talk program.

Now recognized as Tucson's top-rated AM station, KNST is keyed by its affiliation with the UA sports network. From 6:00 to 8:00 p.m. each week night, KNST sparkles as the crown jewel of Tucson sports-talk programming, home to Sports Tonight hosted by Paul Johnson.

"KNST has developed and defined Tucson's sports-talk market. Sometimes now, especially during the school season, there isn't enough time to get to all the callers," says general manager Jerry Misner.

Part of the secret to the popularity of Sports Tonight is that for eight months annually, 20 percent of its programming is Lute Olson and Dick Tomey call-in programs.

KNST has broadcast UA sports since 1980. There are Wildcat fans everywhere, and the Arizona Sports Network reaches them on affiliate stations across the state and into Nevada. Each year more and more Wildcat followers are tuning in to follow the progress of nationally recognized UA teams. From Arizona Stadium, McKale Center, Sancet Field, and sports venues nationwide, the Arizona Sports Network is there to call the action as it happens.

Brian Jeffries is the voice of the Wildcats and director of the Arizona Sports Network. Jeffries joined KNST in 1979. Each year he travels thousands of miles covering Wildcat football, basketball and baseball. Honored annually by the Associated Press, Jeffries keeps his broadcasts fun, fast-moving, and factual.

Other well-liked news and talk shows on KNST are hosted by Tom Snyder, Larry King, Dr. Dean Edell, Paul Harvey, and local talk personality Dale Davidson.

The sister station of KNST is KRQ-FM. Few stations in American radio dominate their respective markets as KRQ dominates Tucson. Every week the station reaches an estimated 183,000 people; that's more than any other Tucson radio station.

ABOVE The voice of the Wildcats, Brian Jeffries wraps up a game with basketball coach Lute Olson.

When KRQ first hit the airwaves in 1979, Linda Ronstadt, the Doobie Brothers and Donna Summer were some of the station's core artists. Today KRQ is still playing the hits—KRQ music is hit music. Current artists such as Amy Grant, Paula Abdul and C + C Music Factory shape the sound of the station.

KRQ also values its involvement in Tucson. The station participates in local fund-raising events such as the Cigna Beau Bridges Tennis Classic; KRQ's Red, White and Boom, Tucson's largest 4th of July celebration; KRQ's Christmas Wish; and the Tucson Open.

"KRQ is an active visible member of the community, and this is extremely important to us," says Misner.

Both KNST and KRQ are owned by Nationwide Communications, Inc.

BELOW Arizona's finest create excitement before a Wildcat game.

Richard Brown never intended to own his own business. His secure job as public relations director for a commercial printing company drove him to it.

"I was utterly and totally bored with what I was doing," he recalls. "I had been doing the same thing for 16 years and I knew all the answers."

In 1977 a local business broker friend persuaded him to consider buying a business in Tucson and moving here from his home in the Los Angeles area.

When Brown and his family came to Tucson to look at the prospects, it was July 4 and blistering hot. After one day they decided there was no way they could live here.

Three days later Brown quit his job and bought Posner's, using his accrued retirement and profit sharing as the down payment.

At the time, Brown knew nothing about art, business, or the art business. But when he saw Posner's, he knew it would be an interesting enterprise.

"I thought Wow! I won't get bored with this business for a long time," says Brown.

His accountant and his lawyer pronounced the store a good buy. Three employees, each of whom had been with Posner's for more than 25 years, were willing to stay on to teach Brown the business.

Posner's was established in 1913 by Philip Posner, a Russian Jewish immigrant. Earning

LEFT Richard Brown is the owner of Posner's Art Store.

POSNER'S ART STORE

his living as a sign painter, Posner found it difficult to obtain the tools necessary to ply his trade in territorial Tucson. He decided to open Posner's as a means of obtaining equipment and also to supply the town with art materials.

During the 1920s the store branched out into house paints and became a Sherwin-Williams dealer. In the late 1940s Posner's began carrying automotive paints.

ABOVE Posner's was established by Philip Posner in 1913 at 233 East Congress Street.

By the 1960s Philip's son, Louie Posner, had taken over the store. When Louie lost the lease on Congress, he moved the store to Park Avenue. Located just outside the main gate of the University of Arizona, Posner's became a second home for UA art and architecture students.

"Students tend to become our children," Brown explains. "Sometimes they are here four and five times a day. We know their names and their families by the time they graduate."

Posner's carries about a half million products—all with their own characteristics—that can be used 10 different ways.

The Park Avenue store is like a student dorm room—messy and interesting. The Oracle Road location, which Brown opened in 1984, is neat and clean and caters to retired people and winter visitors.

PRUDENTIAL SECURITIES INC.

One of the major events in Wall Street history took place in June 1981 when The Prudential Insurance Company of America acquired one of the world's oldest and largest brokerage firms, Bache Halsey Stuart Shields Incorporated.

Bache, as it was informally known, could trace its origin back to 1879. During its long history it exhibited a forward-looking, innovative spirit that made it a leader in a number of investment areas. It was one of the first member firms to make available to its clients mutual funds, commodity futures, spot metals trading, listed options, and life insurance, to name but a few. It was one of the first firms to establish a formal training program for its financial advisors, to install a private news-wire service, and to computerize its operations. All of these and more resulted in comprehensive, efficient, and professional service for the firm's clients.

The largest insurance company in the world, The Prudential brought massive new resources and capabilities to the union, which marked the beginning of a new era in the investment industry. In 1982 the firm's name was changed to Prudential Bache Securities Inc., to reflect the merger of these two distinguished institutions. The firm was renamed Prudential Securities Incorporated in 1991.

Prudential Securities Incorporated serves multiple markets including individuals, institutions, corporations and governments. The firm offers more than 100 products ranging from stocks and bonds and banking services to money management and mutual funds to retirement and estate planning.

Michael F. Digan is vice president and resident manager of the Tucson branch of Prudential Securities. According to Digan, one of the many advantages of working with a local financial advisor is that it keeps the client abreast of local and regional investment issues. The benefit of trading with Prudential Securities is that with more than 300 retail, commodity, institutional and sales offices in 18 countries, the firm has a vast knowledge of the international investment arena.

"When you live in the same economy as your clients, you have a better feel for their needs," says Digan.

According to Digan, the primary function of a financial advisor is to provide clients with every possible assistance in the pursuit of their investment goals. With this in mind, The Prudential Securities Investment Allocation Strategy was designed to provide effective guidance in developing an appropriate investment program that is tailored to the individual. Factors such as age, liquidity needs, cash flow, portfolio size, tax bracket, and, most important, the degree of risk the client is willing to accept in order to achieve investment objectives are taken into consideration when creating such a plan.

ABOVE Prudential Securities serves southern Arizona from its Tucson branch at Williams Centre.

"We are interested in long-range profit planning, not short-term maximum gain," explains Digan, who encourages his clients to take an active role in the investment process.

Prudential Securities Incorporated— it has been rock solid and market wise for more than a century.

The following alumni, friends and supporters from the community have made a valuable commitment to the quality of this project. The publisher and the University of Arizona Department of Intercollegiate Athletics gratefully acknowledge their participation in BEAR DOWN: The University of Arizona, Intercollegiate Sports—A Photographic Chronicle.

"Great Moments" Sponsors

Arizona Technology Development Corporation
Gary Cropper Chevrolet
CyCare Systems
Intergroup Healthcare Corp.
Prudential Securities
Russett Southwest Corporation
Southwest Hazard Control, Inc.
The Tucson Cork, Inc.
Tucson Medical Center
University Medical Center
Westward Look Resort
Weiser Lock
Work Recovery, Inc.

"Partners in Excellence" Contributors

Judith Abrams & Associates, Inc.
Arizona Alumni Association
The Arizona Daily Wildcat
Cat Tracks
Citizens Transfer & Storage
CyCare Systems
Intergroup Healthcare Corporation
Loews Ventana Canyon Resort
The Miles Label Company, Inc.
Miller Bros.
Errol L. Montgomery & Associates, Inc.
940/KNST-AM and 93.7/KRQ-FM
Posner's Art Store
Prudential Securities Incorporated
Rehab Institute of Tucson
Russett Southwest Corporation
Southwest Hazard Control, Inc.
Sundt Corp.
Thomas-Davis Medical Centers
The Tucson Cork, Inc.
University of Arizona
Department of Intercollegiate Athletics
Weiser Lock
Westward Look Resort
The Westin La Paloma
Work Recovery, Inc.

"Quotables" Sponsors

Carl's Jr. of Tucson
Collins-Pina Consulting Engineers, Inc.
A.G. Edwards & Sons, Inc.
Grubb & Ellis, Inc.
Duff and Jim Hearon
Laidlaw Corporation
Lesher and Bordkin, PC
KTVK-TV3
Miller Bros.
S. Jack McDuff & Associates, Inc.
Radisson Suites Hotel
George Rountree
Cox & Russo, PC
Dr. William R. Smitheran
Morris K. Udall, former U.S. Congressman,
2nd District of Arizona
Vision Quest

Patrons

Addison, Roberts & Ludwig, CPA
Allstate Transportation Service
Wm. Anderson Photography
The Arizona Inn
Arizona Travel Center

Arthur Andersen & Co.
Paul Ash Investment Co.
AT&T
Bob Barber, Jr., PC
Baxter Edwards CVS/Terry Gaughan
Beaudry Motor Co.
Larry Berkson
Fred T. Boice
Butler Paper Co.
Carnes Construction, Inc.
Carondelet Health Care
CB Commercial Real Estate
CBS Marketing, Inc.
Robert & Dee Chandler
Chandler, Tullar, Udahl, & Redhair, PC
Cigna Health Plan
Citibank-Arizona
Daniel W. Clarke
Copper Bowl Foundation
Country Club of La Cholla
Deconcini, McDonald, Brammer, Yetwin & Lacy, PC
Delta Products Corporation
Digital Equipment Corporation
Eastlawn/Southlawn Mortuary and Cemetery
A.G. Edwards & Sons, Inc.
Embassy Suites-Airport
Fred Enke
Executive Title Co.
Greg Fahey-State Relations
Farmer John Meats
Frontier Investments, Inc.
Galloway Jeep-Eagle
Tim Garigan
Genesis Machining & Engineering, Inc.
GHMA Medical Centers
Grant Roal Lumber, Inc.
Groundwater Resources Consultants, Inc.
Hazlett & Wilkes, PC
Joe Hernandez Insurance
Holiday Inn-Broadway
Huck Manufacturing, Inc.
Hughes Aircraft Company
Industrial Motor & Control
Intelligent Instrumentation, Inc.
J-Bar-K Enterprises
KPMG Peat, Marwick
Laidlaw Corporation-John Mueller
The Lodge on the Desert
Magma Copper Co.
McGovern, MacVittie, Lodge & Dean, Inc.
Merrill, Lynch, Pierce, Fenner & Smith
Mint Corporation
Modular Mining Systems
The Money Store Investment Corporation
Mueller & Associates
OAE Inc. dba Domino's Pizza
Old Father Inn
Old Pueblo Anesthesia
Paine Webber
Panhellenic Association
Partner's Health Plan of Arizona
Peter Piper Pizza
Quadna, Inc.
Stephen Rodgveller
Rovan, Fahl, Carter Insurance, Inc.
Royal Buick
Russell Russo
The Secretaries
Sergent, Houskins & Beckwith Consulting Geotechnical Engineers
Silo, Inc.
Sonora Desert Hospital
Sunward Materials, Inc.
Tucson Cablevision, Inc.
The Tucson Cork, Inc.
Tucson Electric Power Co.
The University of Arizona
The Wild Catalog
Urban Engineering
US West Communications
Varsity Cleaners & Alterations
Viscount Suite Hotel
Waste Management of Tucson

On the front cover, clockwise from top left: Gymnast Stacy Fowlkes. *Photo: Robert F. Walker. Courtesy, University Photo Center.* Basketball star Sean Elliott. *Courtesy, University of Arizona Athletic Department.* UA legend John "Button" Salmon. *Courtesy, Special Collections, University of Arizona Library.* High jumper Tanya Hughes. *Photo: Tony Duffy/Allsport. Courtesy, University of Arizona Athletic Department.* Wildcat fans. *Photo: Balfour Walker.*

Endpapers, UA fans. *Photo:* Jill Rice.

On the back cover, clockwise from top left: Golfer Manny Zerman. *Courtesy, University of Arizona Athletic Department.* Baseball-great Hank Lieber. *Courtesy, Special Collections, University of Arizona Library.* Volleyball star Melissa "Missy" McLinden. *Photo: Tom Bingham. Courtesy, University Photo Center.* Early basketball team. *Courtesy, Special Collections, University of Arizona Library.* Shortstop Julie Standering. *Courtesy, University of Arizona Athletic Department.* Diver Nancy Kinney MacBeth. *Courtesy, University of Arizona Athletic Department.* Wrestler Gary Rushing. *Courtesy, University of Arizona Athletic Department.*

BEAR DOWN: *The University of Arizona, Intercollegiate Sports—A Photographic Chronicle*
By Janet Mitchell
Photo Consultant and Advisor, Thomas Sanders
Edited by Mary Kirby

Produced in cooperation with the University of Arizona Department of Intercollegiate Athletics. Published by Windsor Publications, Inc., 21827 Nordhoff Street, Chatsworth, CA 91311, (818) 700-0200, with the support of CCA, Inc.

Creative Concept: Author, Janet Mitchell. *Senior Writer:* Jon W. Alquist. *Captions Writer:* Thomas Sanders. *Editor, Profiles:* Jeffrey Reeves. *Profiles Coordinator:* Kelly Goulding. *Assistant,* Keith Martin. *Associate Editors, Profiles:* Michael Nalick, Kevin Taylor. *Proofreaders:* Martha Cheresh, Lin Schonberger. *Editorial Assistant, Profiles:* Kimberly J. Pelletier. *Project Development:* Stewart Weiner. *Managing Editor:* Linda J. Hreno.

Design Concept and Art Direction: Tom Lewis, Inc. *Photo Editor:* Robin L. Sterling. *Production Associate:* Jeffrey Scott Hayes. *Art Production:* Andy Lewis, Amanda Howard. *Art Production Consulting:* Jonathan Wieder.

Windsor Publications, Inc. Elliot Martin, *Chairman of the Board and CEO.* J. Kelley Younger, *Publisher and Editor-in-Chief.* Nellie Scott, *Sales Manager.* Terry Pender, *Controller.*

Library of Congress Cataloging-in-Publication Data
Mitchell, Janet.
Bear down : the University of Arizona, intercollegiate sports—a photographic chronicle / Janet Mitchell.
p. 184 cm. 23 x 31
ISBN 0-89781-428-2
1. University of Arizona—Athletics—History. I. Title.
GV691.U48M58 1992
796'.071'1791—dc20 92-34118
CIP